Fresh Dialogue One

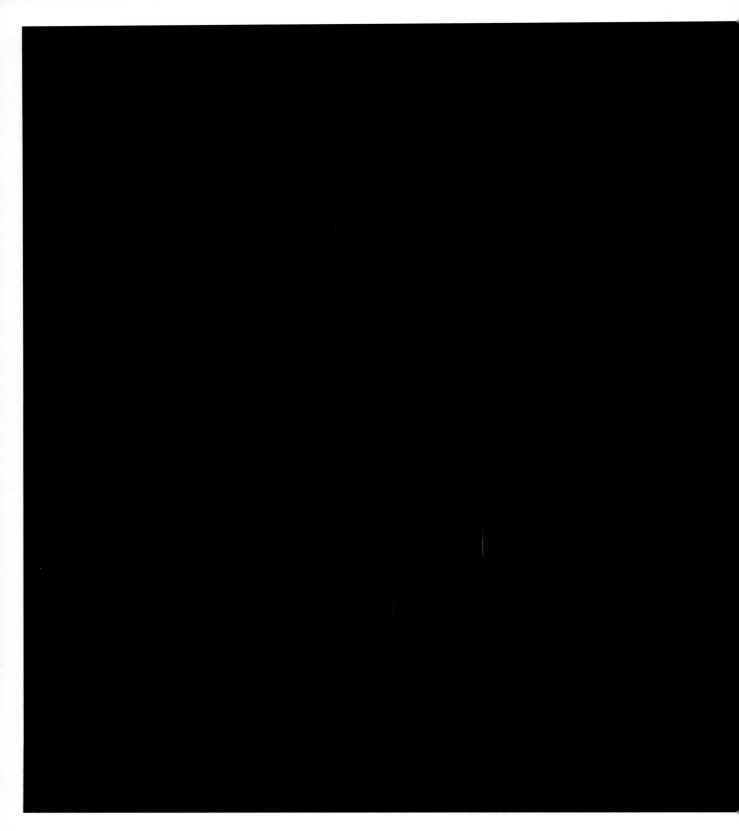

Fresh Dialogue One:
New Voices in Graphic Design

Princeton Architectural Press
American Institute of Graphic Arts—New York

New York

Nicholas Blechman

Christoph Niemann

Paul Sahre

Published by
Princeton Architectural Press
37 East 7th Street
New York, NY 10003
212.995.9620

For a free catalog of books, call 1.800.722.6657
Visit our website at www.papress.com

Project editor: Beth Harrison
Design: Sara E. Stemen
Special thanks to: Ann Alter, Eugenia Bell, Jan Cigliano, Jane Garvie, Caroline Green, Mia Ihara, Clare Jacobson, Leslie Ann Kent,
Mark Lamster, Anne Nitschke, Lottchen Shivers, Jennifer Thompson, and Deb Wood of Princeton Architectural Press
—Kevin Lippert, Publisher

Cover photography by Michael Northrup

Library of Congress Cataloging-in-Publication Data
Blechman, Nicholas.
    Fresh dialogue 1 : New Voices in Graphic Design / Nicholas Blechman, Christoph Niemann, Paul Sahre.
        p. cm.
    ISBN 1-56898-223-2 (pbk.: alk. paper)
    1. Graphic arts—New York (State)—New York—History—20th century. I: Title: Fresh Dialogue One. II: Niemann, Christoph. III: Sahre,
Paul. IV: Title.
    NC975.B57   2000
    741.6'092'27471—dc21   99-053585
                                                                                                                     CIP

Table of Contents

Introduction

In May of 1984, the New York Chapter of the American Institute of Graphic Arts launched a speaker event called "Fresh Dialogue." I was one of the invited speakers that first year, along with David Sterling and Keith Goddard. The goal of the Fresh Dialogue program was to enable the New York design community to hear young, new, or different voices and to experience emerging trends and points of view about graphic design before those ideas became prevalent and mainstream. Hence the word "fresh."

Each year, speakers are recommended and chosen by the AIGA–New York board of directors. There is no pre-selected format for the event, except to allow the individual designers to have a forum to show their work and express their viewpoints. Yet Fresh Dialogue quickly established itself as a highly anticipated annual event that was a sounding board for some of the community's most important voices. A successful speaker is usually transported from the New York stage to the national design lecture circuit.

The list of the Fresh Dialogue speakers now reads like a Who's Who of the American graphic scene. As part of the program, Tibor Kalman addressed the AIGA public for the first time in 1986, Chip Kidd in 1991, and Stefan Sagmeister in 1994. Other past presenters include Jennifer Morla, Rick Valicenti, Barbara Glauber, and Johnathan Hoefler. The list of past years' topics is just as provocative: "Design Without Designers, or How I Learned to Stop Letterspacing and Love the Non-" (1986), "Can Graphic Design Be More Than Pictures of Guys in Suits?" (1990), "Design in the Music Industry" (1994), and "Graphic Activism in Mean Times" (1995).

The 1999 Fresh Dialogue was presented by Nicholas Blechman, Christoph Niemann, and Paul Sahre. I first worked with Nicholas Blechman at the *New York Times* when he assigned me an Op-Ed illustration. I had also been a fan of his underground political publication *Nozone*. Christoph Niemann had briefly worked as my intern at Pentagram years before. He was such a phenomenally talented illustrator and designer that I was embarrassed to ask him to cut a matte. Paul Sahre had shown me his brilliant portfolio of theatre posters when he first moved from Baltimore to New York and I had stayed in touch with him because I admired his work so much.

Upon viewing their work, one might be tempted to characterize Blechman as an art director, Niemann as an illustrator, and Sahre as a designer, but in fact they are each all three of these things. I never thought of them as unit until I saw them together in the same room, as friends and colleagues, and realized there was an obvious, natural, and logical symbiosis among them. All of their work is idea driven, political, humorous, pointed, and biting. In a world of branding, blanding, layering, and obfuscating, they are—excuse the pun—a breath of fresh air.

This Fresh Dialogue evening was held in New York City on May 26, 1999. It was a night to behold. The following book, which documents that event, illustrates why.

Paula Scher
Partner, Pentagram Design
President, AIGA-NY (1998–2000)

Fresh Dialogue One

MEANWHILE

Deserted Kosovar refugee camp, Macedonia. Call: 1 (800) HELP-NOW

NB, CN, PS

American Institute of Graphic Arts
New York Chapter
164 Fifth Ave.
New York, NY 10010

First Class
U.S. Postage
PAID
New York, NY
Permit No. 0000

AIGA/NY Presents: "FRESH DIALOGUE" Featuring: Nicholas Blechman, Christoph Niemann & Paul Sahre

May 26, 1999
Haft Auditorium,
FIT
27th St. & Eighth Ave.
New York City

6:30 p.m. Annual Meeting/
WINE & CHEESE reception
Meet the new board:
Weston Bingham,
Barbara Glauber,
Kent Hunter,
Bonnie Siegler
& Richard Wilde

7:00 p.m. Fresh Dialogue
Three opinionated designers discuss the odd dichotomy between doing graphic design and worrying about Kosovo. They'll address their frequent collaborations as well as the common conceptual threads that run through their very original, very different work.

Admission
AIGA/NY members $10
Non-members $20
Students w/ I.D. $5
(F.I.T. Students Free)

NICHOLAS BLECHMAN

a.k.a. KNICKERBOCKER, is Art Director for The New York Times Op-Ed Page (for which almost every illustrator and designer in the city will drop whatever they're doing for a $100-$300 spot illustration that's due in a few hours), but also works underground as the publisher/editor of the political comics zine "Nozone." He frequently collaborates with Mr. Niemann and Mr. Sahre.

CHRISTOPH NIEMANN

is an illustrator/graphic designer from Germany who lives and works in New York City. In his short time in this country his work has appeared EVERYWHERE (including that very scary portrait of Ken Starr on the cover of The New York Times Magazine). He frequently collaborates with Mr. Blechman and Mr. Sahre.

PAUL SAHRE

is a graphic designer/educator who frequently collaborates with Mr. Blechman and Mr. Niemann. He also oversees the operation of his own one-man design office, where he keeps overhead low and HIGH-PAYING WORK to a minimum, so he can concentrate on doing LOW-PAYING WORK. Mr. Sahre received his BFA and MFA in graphic design from KENT STATE and teaches at The Cooper Union and Parsons School of Design, so you'd think he'd know better. Mr. Sahre is best known for his book jacket and poster design (Fells Point Corner Theatre). He also sits in regularly as Art Director of The New York Times Op-Ed Page.

REGISTER

Register and pay in advance by completing this form and faxing one copy for each attendee to (212) 255-4410.

Name: Ms/Mr _____
Company: _____
Address: _____
City/State: _____
Zip: _____
E-mail: _____
Phone: (___) _____
Fax: (___) _____

☐ AIGA/NY member $10
☐ AIGA/NY student member $5
☐ Non-member $20

Event admission: $ _____
KOSOVO FUND: $$ _____
Membership fees: $ _____

GRAND TOTAL: $$$ _____

Payment method:
☐ Amex ☐ Mastercard ☐ Visa
Card Number _____
Card expiration _____

HELP THE KOSOVO REFUGEES

Make a donation to the International Response Fund, which will help the American Red Cross buy food, clothing, medication and shelter for people in need around the world. The AIGA would be happy to forward your contribution, which you can include with your admission fee. You may also make a donation on the day of the event at the door or contact the American Red Cross directly at 1 (800) HELP-NOW.

BECOME A MEMBER

Become a member of AIGA and add your voice to the design community of New York. The benefits include notification of all programming, discounted entry fees to all events and competitions, a one-year subscription to the AIGA Journal of Graphic Design, and the AIGA National Membership Directory. Professional members also receive AIGA Graphic Design USA, the large-format book documenting the year's competitions, exhibitions and medalists. Members at other levels can purchase a copy at the member's rate.

MEMBERSHIP CATEGORIES

Professional $$$ 255.00
(4 years or more of practice and all employed as service providers to the profession)

Associate $$ 170.00
(Less than 4 years of practice)

Student $ 45.00
(Full-time enrollment only, attach a copy of your current registration receipt)

Group $$$$ 640.00
(Three transferrable professional memberships, owned by a firm or corporation)

Application Fee $ 20.00
(waived for students)

AIGA/NY thanks its annual sponsors:
Mohawk Paper Mills, NY & United Digital Artists, NY

MISSION STATEMENT

The mission of the New York Chapter of the American Institute of Graphic Arts is to identify and define critical issues to its membership and the graphic design profession; to explore and clarify these issues for the purpose of helping to elevate the standards of the business of graphic design; and to create a forum for the exchange of information, views, ideas and techniques among those engaged in the profession.

AIGA/NY Executive Committee 1998-1999

President: Paula Scher
Treasurer: Scott Santoro
Vice Presidents: Georgette Ballance, Annette von Brandis, Sebastian Kaupert, Eric Mueller, Michelle Novak, Dennis Pilsits, Maruchi Santana, Andrew Zolli
Secretary: Angela Reeves
Administrator: Stephen Hinton

212-255-4004
212-255-4410 fax
212-255-4222 DesignLine
www.aigany.org
info@aigany.org

Credits
Chair: Paula Scher
Design: Paul Sahre, Christoph Niemann, Nicholas Blechman
Photography: Bob Cohen Press
Paper: Champion Benefit Mayfair white, 70 lb. text
Thank You(s): Brian Allen, Scott Stowell, Max Bessmann, Joann Gordon, Michelle Shih and James Victore.
Copyright © 1999 AIGANY

NB, CN, PS

SAHRE

We are not going to talk about Kosovo. We
are going to talk about design. But I would
like to say a few things about the poster we
created for this event.

The three of us felt strongly that the
work we do is in context with what's going
on in the world, and that the invitation to
participate in Fresh Dialogue this year was
an opportunity to point out the absurdity we
felt in talking about how much fun we have
making things and how nice this color looks
and how interesting this typeface is or how
wonderful that drawing is while people are
suffering.

Wine and cheese and bombs.

This is a dichotomy that the three of us
are confronted with daily in our work and we
wanted to touch on this with the invitation,
and to raise money and awareness for the
refugees in Kosovo.

BLECHMAN

On to the work.

SAHRE

I work alone, and the last couple of years have been an experiment in keeping overhead low, keeping the level of the work as high as it can be, and taking on the types of projects that interest me—regardless of how much a job pays or does not pay.

I love designing book jackets. With each one of these covers, it's about trying to find whatever the essence of the book is and expressing that graphically. Another thing I like about book jackets is that the subject matter is always changing drastically.

Couplings is a novel about love from the male perspective in pre-unification Germany (right). Designing book jackets, I end up doing a lot of image-making—I guess I would call it—not necessarily traditional illustration. This is usually necessary because of the low budgets, in this case using PhotoShop and Illustrator to create an image.

Omon Ra is a novel satirizing the Russian space program in the late '60s (opposite).

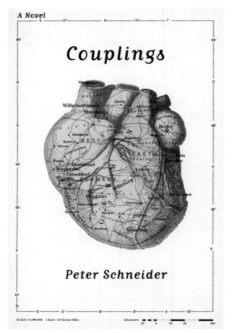

PS

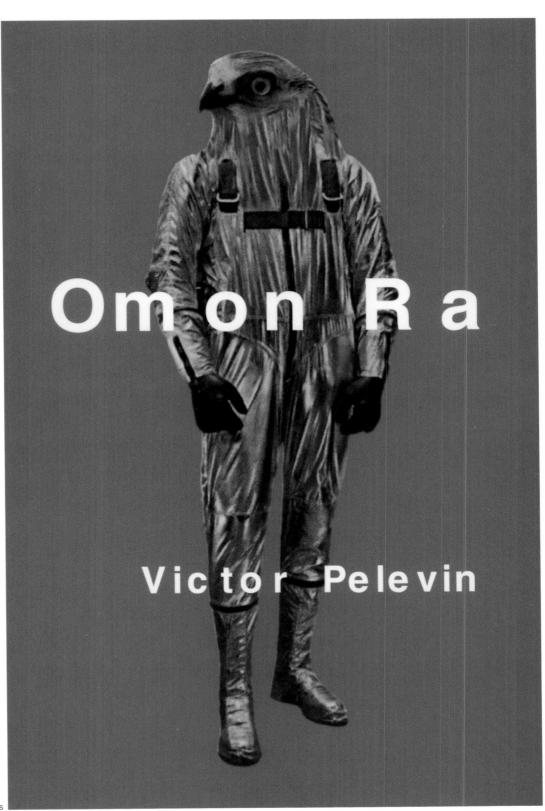

Om on Ra

Victor Pelevin

SAHRE

The Theatre and its Double is a collection of manifestoes originally published in 1938 by Antonin Artaud, a French poet/philosopher who committed suicide in the '50s. On the cover I did an extreme crop of a photograph of Artaud by Man Ray. It's a very intense image, and I felt that by cropping it, I was intensifying it even further. In the book Artaud writes about the state of the theatre at the time and complains about stagnation (this was well before the modern theatre movement). He also compares the theatre to the Plague.

(laughter)

You know, the Black Death, in really disgusting detail. The typography is all scanned from imperfect letterpress printing. It's got that kind of imperfect quality to it.

Why Things Bite Back is a book about how technology, in many ways, makes our lives harder rather than easier.

BLECHMAN

Why did you do the type that way?

SAHRE

I guess for formal reasons: I was trying to echo the plug. But I also wanted it to have the feel of the machine, a default or "unintended" feeling.

Adopt International is a how-to book on adopting children from around the world. As in *Why Things Bite Back*, I hired a photographer, in this case Michael Northrup, to help execute my idea. Here the challenge was to come up with an image that wasn't race- or gender-specific but still said something about the subject matter.

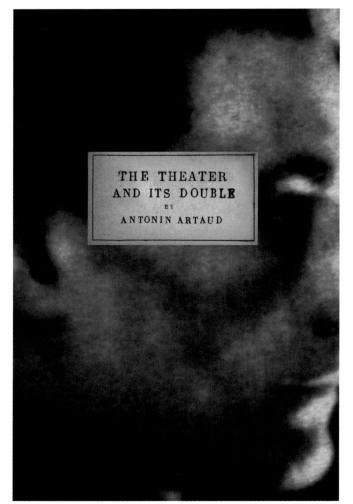

PS

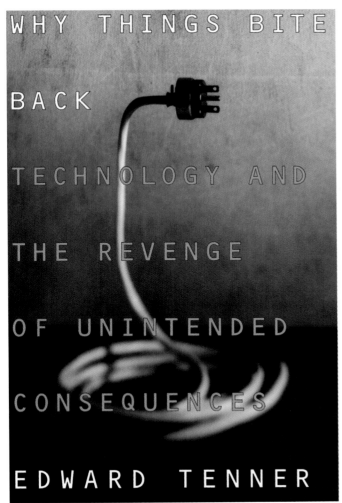

WHY THINGS BITE

BACK

TECHNOLOGY AND

THE REVENGE

OF UNINTENDED

CONSEQUENCES

EDWARD TENNER

PS

ADOPT | *INTERNATIONAL*

Everything You Need to Know *to Adopt*
a Child from Abroad

O. Robin Sweet | *and* | Patty Bryan

PS

On occasion I am able to hire an illustrator. David Plunkert illustrated the cover for this book, *Grey Area*. It's a series of short stories . . . and each of the images represents one of the stories. Very black, black humor. The icon of the guy with the small intestine is for a story called "Scale." It's about a man who has bowel problems. He's taking drugs, and the side effect of the drugs is that he thinks he's shrinking.

Adultery is part self-help book and part novel, and the author says that people eat themselves up when they commit adultery. With the addition of the blue rules, the bedsheets become notebook paper. The handwriting is meant to suggest penance: I will not . . . I will not . . . I will not. . . .

Stripper Lessons is a novel about a man who is obsessed with a stripper.

PS

Adultery

Adultery

Adultery   Ad

Adultery   Adu

~~Adultery~~   Ad

Adultery

Adultery

Louise DeSalvo

PS

★ STRIPPER ★ LESSONS
BY: JOHN O'BRIEN
★ BY THE AUTHOR OF: "LEAVING LAS VEGAS"

PS

This is part of the work that I did when I was a student in Germany. I guess it is a very classical yet surreal approach: taking a face, applying some symbols to it, and trying to create some wit.

I started with one or two and then it turned into 30 or 40 of these drawings, because it was just so fun to do. That was probably the first project that I did where I felt like now I kind of understand what illustration is about, because until I was around 23 I spent all my time drawing very realistically (or at least artistically) but basically without ideas. This was the first thing I did where I felt like I used the drawing to support the idea and didn't just make the drawing for the drawing's sake.

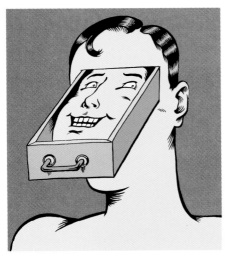
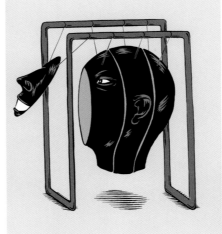

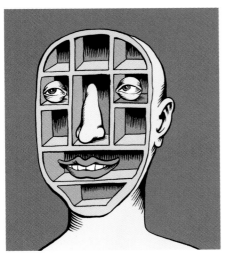
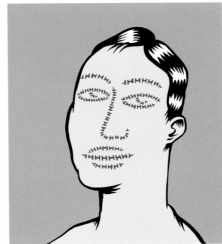
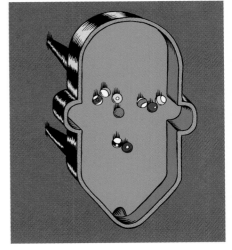

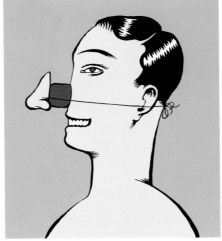

NIEMANN

I met art director Fred Woodward in 1995,
and he offered me a job illustrating Alice in
Chains for *Rolling Stone*. I was of course
freaking out, very nervous, because I was
about to return to Germany and I had only
two days left in New York. And then this guy
calls me up and gives me a job. I should
have told him, I'm leaving, I can't do this."
But of course I told him, "Sure, no problem."
You just don't turn down Fred Woodward.
But everything turned out fine.

    The illustration of Master P, also for
Rolling Stone, is from '97, when I came back
to New York for good. Since then I have done
mostly editorial work. This is another piece
for *Rolling Stone*. Until then I had been doing
my diploma work in Germany, where I tried
to explore different styles and angles. For
my *Rolling Stone* illustrations, it pretty much
always works the same. There isn't really
anything new to say about rock and roll. So I
just draw a big face and combine it with a
weird idea. I don't know if Master P is really
a gangster rapper, but he's definitely a
tough guy.

BLECHMAN

The *New York Times* would never publish
that.

NIEMANN

Why not? He has glasses. He looks intellec-
tual. So maybe they would go for it.

    This is the singer of Prodigy, he has that
weird hair (opposite right).

CN

CN

One thing that I like to do is to come up with an idea and then find the appropriate style. With all these articles about the Internet there are a lot of chances to use a pixelated style. This illustration was for a piece on turkey recipes on the Internet (top right).

The next illustration was something for the *New Yorker* on a guy being in an almost *1984*-type Big-Brother office world (bottom right).

The *New Yorker* has this little column on books, and this illustration (far right, top) deals with letter conversations. I feel like, in this case, a really slick computer style wouldn't work. These I always try to draw more classically, more charmingly.

CN

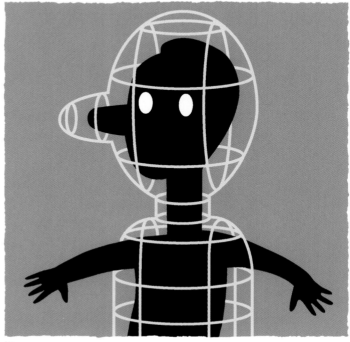

CN

CN

CN

NIEMANN

I also like to paint, like with this piece for the *New York Times Book Review* on genealogy and Mendel (top right).

That's for the National Post, a piece about the history of Chile in the '70s and '80s (bottom right).

BLECHMAN

How long were you taking to execute these?

NIEMANN

It depends. Here, the final execution for the drawing itself might have been 15 minutes. The actual drawing is probably only 15 lines, so it's not the hardest thing, but putting it together, choosing the colors, then changing the separations—that's what's time-consuming with this technique.

For the Book Review, the actual drawing has to go pretty fast because otherwise it gets too stiff pretty soon. This was great opportunity because here I could do the entire issue (all together 20 illustrations) and I could come up with the style. When I was a student they'd always tell you, "It doesn't happen. You just don't get these jobs where people ask you to come up with something visually entertaining for a publication with so much exposure."

BLECHMAN

In Germany, maybe.

NIEMANN

Yeah, I know, but also in the States it's a very rare opportunity to get such a big space—and here I could even do the type, which apparently never happened before. The *Times* won't usually change the *Book Review* logo—they tend to be very rigid about that. I developed these characters for the cover, and they also appear with the inside illustrations.

CN

CN

Book Review

Summer Reading

Like this one for the Travel section (right).
They are all the basic comic characters.

I also did some animated movies and I like
this thing where you play with a mixture of
animation and comic strips but where you
still have illustration in panels (opposite,
top). It's not supposed to be "real" comic
that you read with a funny end or a real
story. It's really meant to be one illustration
that has 20 or 30 panels. It works like one
image, and if you read it you get a second
layer.

BLECHMAN

Do you ever drop your ink like that?

SAHRE

That happens to you all the time, right?

NIEMANN

Oh, yeah. I did it two weeks ago, and before
that I had a year where I didn't and it was
the first year in my life. Usually I do it on a
two-month basis. And I have a black table
now, which helps a lot, so it's not such a big
disaster.

That's an inside piece from a Parsons School
of Design catalogue on illustration and
advertising (opposite, bottom left). It's nice
when you can use a few panels to develop a
story without explaining it in type.

That's a piece from the same catalogue, on
floral design (opposite, bottom right).

CN

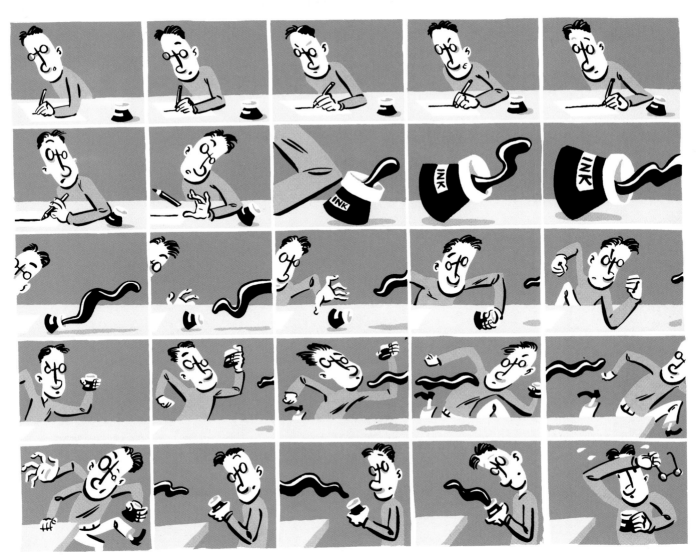

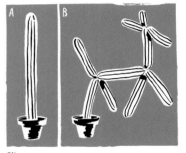

This is my first publication, *Surge* (right). It was inspired by Art Spiegelman's *Raw* and the punk DIY 'zine movement. It was copublished with my brother Max under the pseudonyms of Domino Knox and Knickerbocker because we were afraid of being blacklisted by the FBI for our radical views. He was the editor and I was the art director, and we would always get into fights because he wanted more articles and I wanted more comics. So he went on to do *Drunken Boat*, a radical literary journal, and I founded *Nozone*, a comics 'zine (opposite). My grandmother is a communist, my mother is an ecologist, and my brother is a romantic anarchist, so it's understandable that my first efforts in self-publishing would have a political nature. Originally conceived as an ecological comix zine (the name of the magazine is a pun on the state of the enviornment) the first issue was devoted to air pollution.

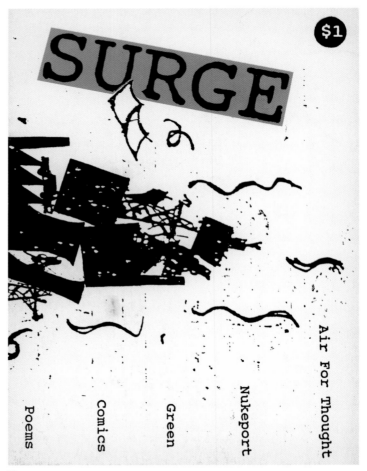

NB

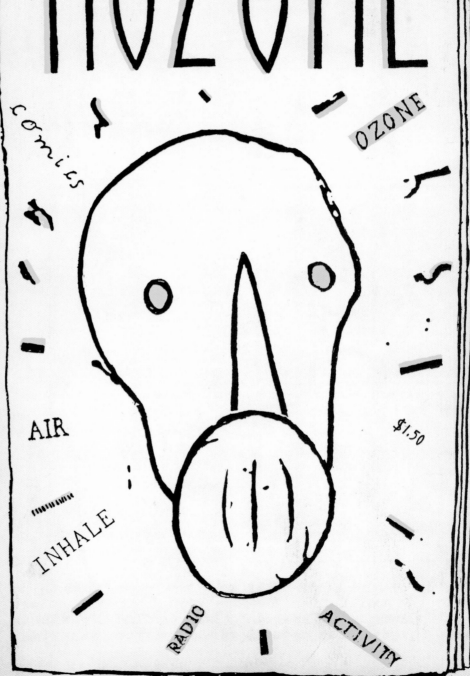

BLECHMAN

This is a spread from *Nozone* #1. It satirizes
Bush's claim that he was the Environmental
President. Here, he's vacuuming up protesters.

NB

tal President: "Why sure I'm cleaning up!"

BLECHMAN

The first issue was printed on a web press. There was a red Xerox cartridge in my father's animation studio where I was operating out of, and I used it to create an accordion-fold strip, which I then pasted into each of the 1,000 issues.

Gas masks are a kind of leitmotif used throughout the magazine. Ron Barrett used the combination of a gas mask pamphlet and a vacuum cleaner manual for this montage (opposite, right).

NB

NB

BLECHMAN

A year later I came out with *Nozone* #2.
I decided that no true underground publication looked the same twice, so I changed theme and format from issue to issue. This oblong shaped issue's semiacademic theme is "The Idea of Nature." The two-color craft-paper cover is by Gary Baseman (right).

The theme for *Nozone* #3 is war. Dubbed "Special Destruction Dispatch," this was the magazine that was supposed to stop the Gulf War, but it didn't come out until three months after the war ended. The cover is by Joost Swarte with an orange belly band pasted around the front (opposite left). To this day people are most impressed with the fact that I hand-pasted 2,000 of these around each issue. All the lettering is done by hand, and a lot of the art is pick up art, using the Xerox machine, rummaging for images in the picture collection of the New York Public Library, collaging things together.

The issue ran into all sorts of problems because of its awkward size. Many distributors refused to carry it because it wouldn't fit on conventional bookshelves, and couldn't be shipped in standard boxes.

NB

26

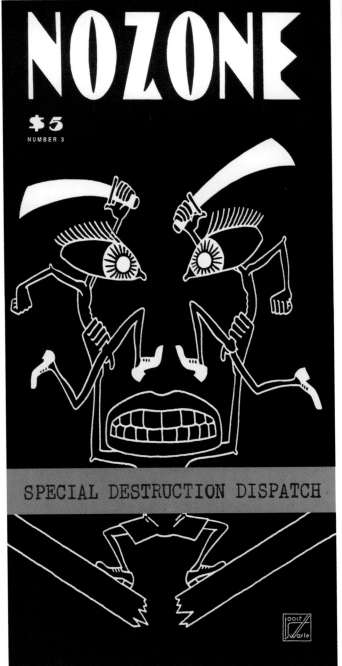

BLECHMAN

I decided to come out with a more economic
format for the next issue. *Nozone* #4, the
"Utopia" issue, is a perfect square (below).
For the Utopia issue I actually went to
a small town in Texas called Utopia. I photo-
graphed the town and juxtaposed that with
quotes from H.G. Wells (opposite).

NUMBER 4 UTOPIA / DYSTOPIA

The dreams of artists, of perfect and lovely bodies and of a world transfigured to harmony and beauty had been realized; the spirits of order and organization ruled triumphant.

For indeed [this] was the Promised Land of human desires.

Here at last established and secure, were peace, power, health, happy activity, length of days and beauty.

All that we seek was found here and every dream was realized.

NB

In the mid '90's I came out with *Nozone* #5, "Poverty Comix." There was talk of an economic recession, and the streets of New York were filled with homeless.

Subtitled "Hard Strips for Hard Times," this is the back cover (opposite, left). The "Made in U.S.A." labels were a take on 1930s nationalism, but I had it printed in Toronto and it wouldn't pass over the border unless I had the words "Printed in Canada" at the bottom.

"Americans will have to make sacrifices to rebuild the economy and reduce the national debt" was something that Clinton was saying when he was running for his first term. So I thought, Why not show people who've really made sacrifices for their country: war veterans.

NB

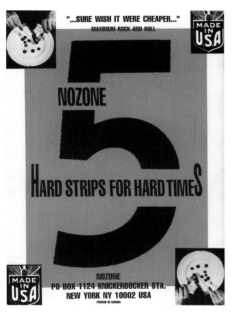

NB

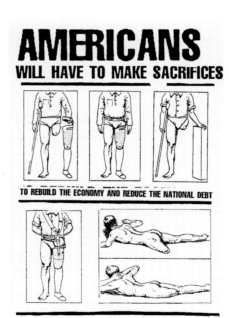

NB

NB

This was an attempt to sell magazines, right? How long did it take for you to start thinking in these terms, and what about distribution?

BLECHMAN

Part of the trick of self-publishing is getting it out there. At a certain point it becomes a product. And *Nozone* is especially difficult to market because it keeps changing size, is published on a sporadic schedule, and the masthead never stays the same. Imagine trying to find the *New Yorker* at a newsstand but you don't know what it looks like or when it comes out.

Some distributors would help me; they would say, "Why don't you do a flier. We need a flier to help sell this." So I had my intern, Mike Gorman, design this promo for *Nozone* #5. Another thing I learned about distribution is that, instead of returning unsold copies, some distributors throw them out and send back an affidavit certifying the number of copies not sold. And then at the bottom of the slip would be "method of destruction," either "incineration," "recycling," or the more progressive distributors would donate them to prisons. Before the affidavit system they would simply tear the masthead off the front covers so I would get a stack of torn-up covers as proof that they didn't sell. Which was always a horrible moment because I put so much into each issue—really, it was just awful.

This is a comic strip I did (opposite). There's nothing to say about it, except for the fact that nobody else would publish me at the time so the easiest way to get started was to publish myself. In a way, that attitude motivated the whole magazine. If I couldn't get things published elsewhere the way I wanted, then I would publish them myself.

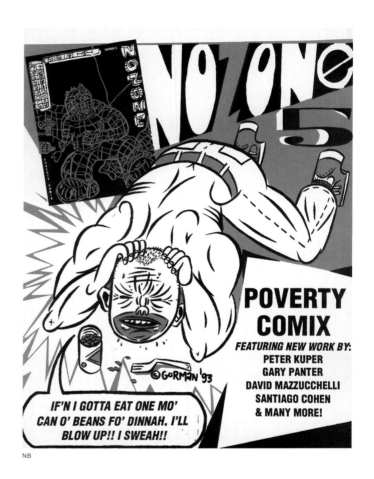

NB

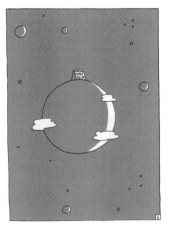

NB

SAHRE

And pay for it yourself.

BLECHMAN

Which upset my parents. I was always broke.

SAHRE

Great cover.

BLECHMAN

Really?

NIEMANN

At first when I saw it I was so impressed with the entire publication. I thought Knickerbocker was 20 great underground American illustrators doing this magazine together because there was no address, there was just a P.O. Box somewhere in New York. And it was like, Oh, that is what they're doing in their spare time. I never thought it was just one guy doing the entire thing. I still love it graphically, and the general idea is great.

BLECHMAN

Thanks.

This is *Nozone* #6, the "Crime" issue. The two-color cover is by David Mazzucchelli (opposite). The word "*Nozone*" is so small that most thought it was a new magazine called "*Crime.*"

Chip Kidd and Calvin Chu did this piece (top right). I didn't know it at the time, but I was developing a style for how I would do the New York Times Op-Ed page. I would ask graphic designers, cartoonists, photographers, and illustrators to contribute. So it wasn't necessarily a comics 'zine. It kind of crossed borders to create some strange graphic hybrid.

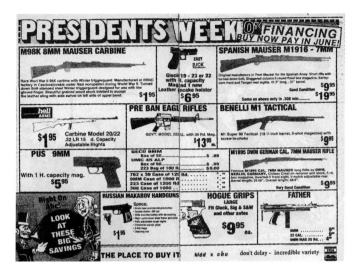

NB

Nozone #7, the "Extremism" issue, was inspired by the Oklahoma City bombing and the proliferation of right-wing militias across the country. Printed in camouflage colors, the back cover (opposite, top left) is an ironic homage to the religious right.

More than anything else, *Nozone* was a showcase for underground talent and an opportunity for illustrators to work outside the constraints of the commercial world. Artists would work for free, but in exchange would get free copies.

At this point I started working for the *Times* and I realized that I needed help putting the next issue of *Nozone* together.

NB

EKSTREAMYSM

EQCTHFUMOSM

EXTREMISM

$7

Nicholas and I met in Williamsburg, Brooklyn. We got together one night and started talking and we realized that we had a lot in common as far as how we work and what we were interested in. And he showed me issues 1 through 7 of *Nozone* and I told him I'd love to get involved in any way.

So he asked me to design the next issue.

The theme of *Nozone* #8 is "Work." This is the cover (opposite).

It's a one-color magazine with a belly band containing all the information about the issue. So, when you take the band off, there's really nothing on the cover: no title, no price, etc.

Nicholas is always into experimenting as far as how this thing is going to happen on the newsstands. We felt that there's so much confusion on the newsstands, the way to get people to pay attention to our magazine is to put nothing on the cover. And, therefore, its inactivity would make it something that people would pay attention to. After we finished this it went out to the distributors and it was in stores. I remember going to a store that I knew carried the magazine—St. Mark's Books—to look around for it, but I couldn't find it. I thought, Maybe it hasn't been shelved yet or whatever. I looked for the thing for 15 minutes, and just couldn't find it. I finally asked and it turned out to be pretty much everywhere in the store. It was in four different, prominent areas. It was even outside in the front window. But for some reason, I just couldn't see it. I don't know if it was my over-familiarity with it or what, but it was invisible to me. It was like it had a cloaking device on it.

(laughter)

NOZONE # 8: WORK

PLEASE CROSS OUT PRECEDING ADDRESS.
USE UNTIL ALL SPACES ARE FILLED.

$10

NAME	NAME	NAME
DEPT.	DEPT.	DEPT.
NAME	NAME	NAME
DEPT.	DEPT.	DEPT.
NAME	NAME	NAME
DEPT.	DEPT.	DEPT.

BLECHMAN

The invisible magazine.

SAHRE

It was crazy.

NIEMANN

That's what an underground magazine is all about. That's real underground!

Blechman

We kind of undermined ourselves

SAHRE

Yeah, we did.

Blechman

We shot ourselves in the foot with how underground it was.

SAHRE

Yeah.

BLECHMAN

But that was the whole idea.

SAHRE

We put all the information—title, price, etc.—on the back cover so that in case the belly band was removed or lost, stores could put it on the shelves with the back cover showing. That was the idea anyway.

NO

MANUFACTURED AND MARKETED BY NOZONE, A DIVISION OF NODESIGN, NYC 1998.

Made in U.S.A.

Z ON
E #8

PM 5 00

NB, PS

"This is just an in-between job."
—*American Airlines* Stewardess.

NOZONE

Pre-publication mail

Dear Nozone—It is a big mistake to think that WORK has existed since the beginning of time. It is actually a rather new development in human history. Animals don't work (unless humans have gotten to them), and we didn't either until the advent of agriculture. The Bushmen, for example, don't work even today. Nor do many tribes in places like New Guinea. They hunt, fish and gather - but they do not consider these activities any different from eating, fucking, playing, fighting, living. WORK is a modern idea. And the concept of working for someone other than oneself and one's immediate tribe or family dates from the day before yesterday.
Cheers. —Harry Gordon

"No one should ever work...Almost all evil you'd care to name comes from working or from living in a world designed for work. In order to stop suffering, we have to stop working."—Bob Black

RANKS THE HIGHEST AMONG MAGAZINES WITH THE LOWEST DISTRIBUTION, SELLING A SLIM 1300 COPIES IN 1997, DOWN FROM 2200 IN 1994. WE RECENTLY LOST SEVERAL MAJOR DISTRIBUTORS DUE TO MARKETPLACE PRESSURES, AND HAVE NO ECONOMIC REASON TO CONTINUE PUBLICATION.

WORLD LEADERS REFUSE TO HEAR OUR PLEAS. IN OUR FIRST ISSUE, WE EXPOSED THE WRETCHED STATE OF THE ENVIRONMENT ONLY TO DISCOVER THAT IT HAS CONTINUED TO DETERIORATE. IN OUR SPECIAL "DESTRUCTION DISPATCH" WE ATTACKED THE MILITARY ESTABLISHMENT, YET SEVEN WARS HAVE BEEN WAGED WORLDWIDE SINCE THEN. IN OUR "UTOPIA" ISSUE (#4), WE OFFERED OUR VISIONS OF A BETTER WORLD ONLY TO FIND THAT THE ONE WE LIVE IN HAS GOTTEN WORSE. IN "POVERTY COMICS" (#5), WE ATTACKED MULTI-NATIONAL CONGLOMERATES FOR CREATING A NEW CLASS OF WORKINGPOOR. SINCE THEN THE POVERTY RATE HAS GONE UP. IN 1996, OUR "CRIME ISSUE" (#6) CHALLENGED CONVENTIONAL NOTIONS OF CRIME, GLORIFYING PETTY THIEVERY AND ARMED REBELLION. YET TO OUR DISMAY, CRIME HAS GONE DOWN.

Publisher, Editor and Plant Manager: Knickerbocker
Guest Designer: Paul Sahre
Special Agent; Supervisor, Text Department: Jesse Gordon
Thanks to Aida Edemariam, Dan Freidlaender, Kerrylyn Genevive and Jonathon Rosen.

Nozone is an independently published graphic anthology of critical thinking that, in an era of political and social despair, finds meaning in a well drawn comic.

Printed by The Studley Press, P.O. Box 214 Dalton MA 01226

Copyright © 1998 all contributors. Nozone, P.O. Box 1124 Knickerbocker Station, New York, NY, 10002, USA.

WE THEN LAUNCHED OUR "EXTREMISM" ISSUE (#7), INJECTING HEAVY DOSES OF LEFTIST PRAGMATISM INTO THE PSYCHOTIC RELIGIOUS RIGHT ONLY TO FIND THEM IMMUNE TO OUR PRESCRIPTION. DESPITE THESE SETBACKS (AND BECAUSE OF THEM) WE ARE DETERMINED TO FIGHT ON, FUELED BY RAGE, AN IRRATIONAL HOPE FOR SOCIAL JUSTICE, AND LARGE DOSES OF RED WINE.

WELCOME TO NOZONE #8

WORK

THE "WORK" ISSUE WAS MADE INEVITABLE BY THE FACT THAT THE EDITOR NOW HAS A FULL TIME JOB (COMPLETE WITH WATER COOLER, OFFICE POLITICS, AND UNPAID OVERTIME); BY THE FACT THAT WORK CONSUMES A THIRD OF ONE'S LIFE (AN OPTIMISTIC FIGURE); AND BY THE AWARENESS THAT WORK IS A UNIVERSAL CONDITION, THE SOUL OF CAPITALISM, THE ENEMY OF LEISURE, AND THE CAUSE OF REVOLUTIONS. THE "WORK" ISSUE IS DIVIDED INTO THREE SECTIONS CORRESPONDING TO THE THREE PARTS OF THE DAY: "BEFORE WORK", "DURING WORK", AND "AFTER WORK". THE "DURING WORK" SECTION TELLINGLY RECEIVED THE MOST SUBMISSIONS.

—THE EXECUTIVE BOARD OF NOZONE

"I'm a humor columnist. I don't have anything funny to say about being a humor columnist."
—Humor Columnist; Lafayette, IN.

"I actually look forward to going to work lots of times. It sort of helps to pass the time sometimes."—Record Store Employee; NYC

Contributors

Steven Ahlgren	9:00 AM	David Plunkert	12:49 PM
	10:00 AM	Brian Rea	1:03 PM
Hammermil Fore DP	12:00 PM	Particle 17	1:17 PM
	4:00 PM	Takeshi Tadatsu	2:41 PM
Gary Baseman	9:12 AM	P. Revess	2:56 PM
Mark Marek	10:05 AM	Blex Bolex	3:11 PM
Lohrow		Ron Barrett	4:12 PM
Knickerbocker	10:12 AM	Scott Stowell	4:12 PM
Ed Subitzky	10:25 AM	Johnny Sweetwater	4:23 PM
Johnathon Rosen	10:45 AM	Gary Clement	4:34 PM
Lloyd Dangle	11:09 AM		
Christoph Niemann	11:23 AM		
Benoit	11:36 AM		
Paul Sahre	11:46 AM		

"My favorite season of work is Spring, only because I find people are generally more content ... and because I'm a Therapist and a Bartender, that makes me happy."
— Therapist/Bartender, NYC

"Work, in economics and sociology, the activities necessary to the survival of society."
— *Encyclopedia Britannica*, 15th Edition

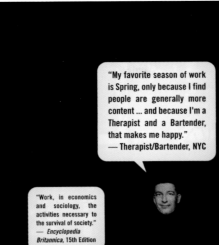

THE NOZONE
WORK
QUESTIONNAIRE

In the interest of "taking the temperature" of our national workforce, the Nozone Editorial Board has prepared the attached 'WORKERS' SURVEY'. We ask you to please take 10 or 15 minutes to complete the questionnaire. We assure you that your answers will remain completely confidential, so please answer freely and without self-censorship. Results will be printed in the next issue of Nozone — although, if our hunch is right, the repercussions of this survey will be felt in the GLOBAL ARENA well before this date.

- HOW DOES YOUR MISERY MEASURE UP TO EVERYONE ELSE'S?
- ARE YOU AS ALONE AS YOU FEEL?
- IS YOUR ANGER JUSTIFIED?
- DOES OUR SYSTEM NEED TO BE COMPLETELY RENOVATED?

We need to know.

CHECK OUT BACK ISSUES
◄— OF NOZONE

Supplies are limited for these classic back issues: Extremism, Poverty Comix, and Utopia-Dystopia.

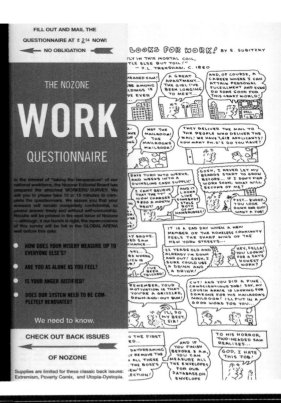

The History of Work

The history of work is a history of conflict. There were two industrial revolutions: that of the industrialist imposing new means of **mechanization** upon the worker, and that of the worker protesting these new means. It is this second revolution, buried in history books and erased from this nation's collective memory, that needs exhuming. **American workers in the mid-nineteenth century, at the onset of industrialization, were fucked.** In coal mines, cotton mills, steel plants, and railroads, work was characterized by miserable pay, long workdays, and injury. In New York, working class families lived in one room, cholera-infested apartments with no plumbing or garbage removal. In New Hampshire factory managers would set the clocks back to get more hours from their workers. In Massachusetts, shoemakers worked sixteen-hour days at **$3 a week.** Such **abuse** led to strikes, which brought in the police and the National Guard, which led to bloodshed, violence, and further oppression. The workplace became a battlefield. On the surface workers fought for higher wages and shorter hours, but underneath there lurked a naive yet genuine sense that if the working class gained control of the nation's resources, life would improve. Such idealism led to an unprecedented wave of violence. Mills were set ablaze, trains derailed, machines unbelted, rocks thrown and guns fired. Between 1860 and 1906 there were thirty-eight thousand **strikes** and **lockouts.** Unions became to workers what the army is to soldiers: organized fighting forces in the war between capital and labor. The strength of the unions was such that, by the beginning of the nineteen hundreds, after half a century of violence,

> "War factories must be kept operating at capacity. America's idle womanpower must be mobilized. This is the message to be voiced to the women of America by motion pictures."—*Office of War Information to Hollywood,* 1942

> "O, I like my boss / He's a good friend of mine / That's why I'm starving / Out in the breadline." —*The Little Red Songbook*

came an era of reform in which **big business** made certain concessions in order to blunt the edge of labor. It was an attempt to stabilize the ship while sailing over troubled waters. Though anger persisted through the twenties and the thirties, the forties brought the war economy, and with it enough prosperity to quell the **rage of the workers** and destroy the labor movement. War became the national job for which everyone worked. The war economy was so profitable that it was continued after the war had been won. The communist threat brought high wages and stability, **replacing conflict with cushiness.** America had won the war abroad, and big business had won the war at home. The fifties were the Golden Age of labor relations, determined largely by collective bargaining. Because the gains of collective bargaining were negotiated privately (through contracts) and not publicly (through law) they were subordinate to the will of industry. During the sixties, industry successfully lured workers from unions to the side of management, thus undermining union stability. This de-unionization accelerated in the seventies with plant relocation to non-organized areas, employer illegality (between 1978 and 1979 there were 30,000 cases of unfair labor practice) and the **failure of unions** to organize in emerging businesses (such as the computer chip industry). The election of Reagan brought not only the end of the Golden Age, but the full scale defeat of labor. During his 'recovery' (the first economic boom not accompanied by an increase in wages) **every single law or institution designed to protect workers was dismantled.** Globalization, deregulation, and automation, rendered labor powerless against the united front of industry.

> "I was there in Pittsburgh in '77 among the railroad men. Somebody filled an engine and five carsful of oil, set it afire, and run it forty miles an hour into the round house where the Pinkertons was livin'. It was a patch a' hell sizzlin' in its own juice."
> — Worker on the strikes of 1877

NB, PS

SAHRE

This is a center spread, with a little book tipped-in (right).

BLECHMAN

A little-book-within-a-bigger-book kind of thing.

NIEMANN

It's great.

SAHRE

This is the first piece Nicholas showed me after I agreed to get involved with *Nozone* (opposite).

NIEMANN

What I like about this piece in particular is that it's not illustration, it's not a comic strip, it's not writing. It's something between those things. I feel that *Nozone* is the only stage for stuff like this, where it really makes sense, where it doesn't look strange.

SAHRE

The main character, Steve, designs roofing sealants and is having problems on the job. As it turns out, Steve is not suffering from work-related stress, but is just a drug addict. Very funny. It's by Sabin Streeter and is illustrated with really bad clip art.

These photographs are all by Steve Algren. We asked him to use some of these images in the magazine and he agreed.

NB, PS

NB, PS

SAHRE

At this point Nicholas has gotten his
process down as far as how he begins an
issue. He has a formal call-for-entries letter
that he sends out to illustrators and designers who have submitted work in the past or
whom he is trying to get to participate for
the first time.

Nozone was my first exposure to Christoph's
work (opposite). Nicholas would drop off
new submissions as they came in. He'd
come to my studio, or we'd meet for a beer
or whatever. On one occasion, he sent me a
package. After opening it, I called Nicholas
and asked him, What's with this Hitler
thing? Nicholas explained that it was by an
illustrator named Christoph Niemann and
that Christoph was German. Then it all made
sense in this weird way. Or maybe a not-so-
weird way.

9 GREAT JOBS
IF YOU FAIL TO BECOME A DICTATOR

MUSEUM EMPLOYEE

TREE

ACTOR

MECHANIC

WIND-SHIELD-WIPER

DIVER

RAILROAD-
ASSISTANT

GAMBLER

UNEMPLOYED

NIEMANN

I change my idea about how appropriate my symbols are on a daily basis.

This is "The Good Portrait." It was the first book that I got published. It's 65 portraits of famous people and the portrait is actually a computer icon—32 by 32 pixels. The drawings aren't fancy because they're just pixels that are drawn on the computer with the mouse. There's nothing artistic about it. And there's nothing funny about it because the symbols themselves aren't supposed to be funny. The names are just names of people that are famous in some way and the fun only happens when you read the symbol and you connect this in your head. I don't know how profound my knowledge is of culture and art and everything. Probably this is as far as it goes. But maybe it makes it easier to make jokes about stuff you don't know too much about yourself.

BLECHMAN

Is this what you were showing to get your first jobs? This is the first stuff that I saw of yours.

NIEMANN

Yeah. This is what I had in my book. This is how I prepared for America.

(laughter)

NIEMANN

The funny thing for me is . . .

SAHRE

A lot of them are crappy American characters.

NIEMANN

Yes, for example, Shakespeare. No, Shakespeare was Canadian, I think.

(laughter)

CHURCHILL   NIXON

BATMAN   NAPOLEON

CHRISTO   PICASSO   MALEWITSCH   TOULOUSE-LAUTREC

MUNCH   ARCIMBOLDO   BASELITZ   GIACOMETTI

SHAKESPEARE   MUHAMMAD ALI   PELE   CYRANO DE BERGERAC

ATLAS   THE THREE WISE MEN   SHERLOCK HOLMES   RENE MAGRITTE

E.T.　　PYRRHUS　　NERO　　JOHN W. BOBBIT　　STEVIE WONDER　　BEETHOVEN　　THE MARATHON MAN

ARCHIMEDES　　HOROWITZ　　JUDAS　　MICHELANGELO　　EVE　　PAMELA ANDERSON　　KATE MOSS

BOCUSE　　POSEIDON　　HITCHCOCK　　KÖNIG ARTHUS　　JACQUES COUSTEAU　　NARCISSUS　　MOSES

ICARUS　　OBLOMOV　　REINHOLD MESSNER　　JESUS　　ASTERIX　　OBELIX　　IDEFIX

CAIN　　ABEL　　ROMEO　　JULIET　　SIEGFRIED　　UND ROY　　GODOT

PONTIUS PILATE　　ST. MARTIN　　ARIADNE　　DIOGENES　　SYSIPHOS　　BRUCE LEE　　MURPHY

CN

49

NIEMANN

It was really amazing to see how well everything works here in America and I actually feel that going to Paris or London would have been harder for me even though geographically those places are a lot closer to Germany. And New York is so similar to Germany. I don't know if I was so much exposed to American culture but the symbols I used and also the way I presented them took so little explanation. It seems that the thinking and the humor are very similar and so I never felt that there was a cultural gap that I had to cross.

Also, the fun of doing this really simple stuff is that you can just take high art and whatever is considered low art and, by putting them next to each other, you reduce them to similar things. And therefore make a statement that might be a little bit beyond just jokes.

This is something I did for *Entertainment Weekly* (opposite). It's about the Oscar race. That year everything was about *Shakespeare in Love*. So I took this Hamlet idea and made a play with that for Best Actor, Best Supporting Actor, Best Actress, and Best Picture. It's supposed to get funnier the more you see it, or the more you see the symbol being changed. It's not only about this illustration but it's about the one before it—how it changes and how this new one adds to the meaning.

CN

Talking of symbols, this is the *Praying Hands* by Albrecht Dürer, which is probably the most famous drawing in Germany (top right). You find it in every second household. I was doing a book called *The Good Drawing* and I was thinking that the preaching hands are *the* good drawing. Dürer did me a good favor by leaving a lot of blank space around it—you can easily add things. And I felt that if the preaching hands are a 100% good drawing, if you add stuff, you can easily get 110 or 120%, which might be even better. So the next five drawings are what I think you could add to the preaching hands (bottom row, and opposite).

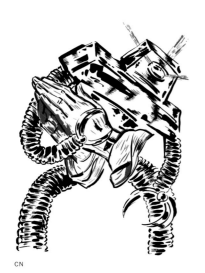

CN

CN

CN

This is a poster that I silkscreened for the
Baltimore chapter of the AIGA (opposite).
They needed something that was kind of
special, that they could give people who
donated money or helped the AIGA in some
way. And my thinking was that they're
always thanking these people but they're
always begging them to help again next
year. So, this is an oversized silkscreen
poster of, essentially, the Dürer hands praying and then clapping.

Using Christoph's formula, I figured that
the artist who drew this set of hands
decreased the value to about 60% (right). I
added perhaps 20% back, so the poster total
is 80%.

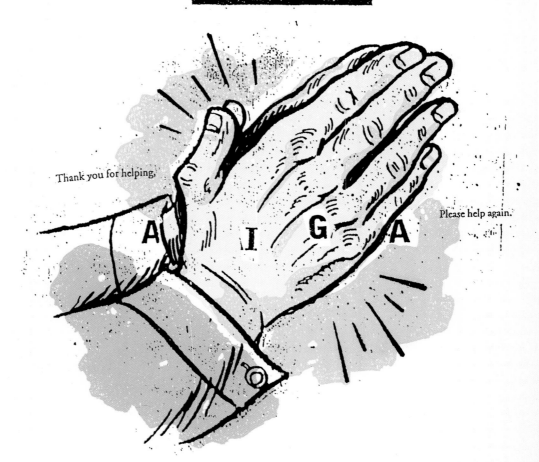

APPLAUD

Thank you for helping.

Please help again.

IMPLORE

SAHRE

I mentioned silkscreening a few posters. I moved to Baltimore after graduate school and took a job at a marketing communications firm. On the whole it was an awful job—unrewarding corporate work, annual reports, etc. To keep my sanity, I set up a crude silkscreen studio in my basement as a means of producing work I was interested in, and as an extension of some work I was doing as a graduate student at Kent State University.

The ceiling was very low in that basement, so I always had to crouch down. All the equipment was homemade. I didn't have a drying rack so I ran a clothesline with clothespins instead. The rinsing tray was also handmade. It had hole at the bottom and was fitted with a tube. The water from the rinsing tray would flow out this tube and into a five-gallon bucket. You really don't need much equipment to silkscreen.

BLECHMAN

Was it always lit like a disco?

SAHRE

No, no, it was a typical basement. This is a photograph by Michael Northrup, who used a strobe technique with colored gels. I guess Michael and I thought the space needed some glamour.

These are some of the posters I printed in my studio (pages 58–59).

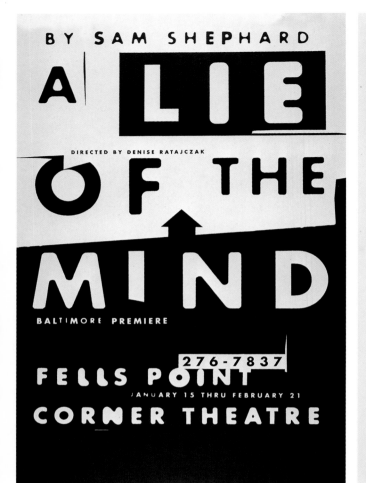

BY SAM SHEPHARD

A LIE OF THE MIND

DIRECTED BY DENISE RATAJCZAK

BALTIMORE PREMIERE

276-7837

FELLS POINT

JANUARY 15 THRU FEBRUARY 21

CORNER THEATRE

PS

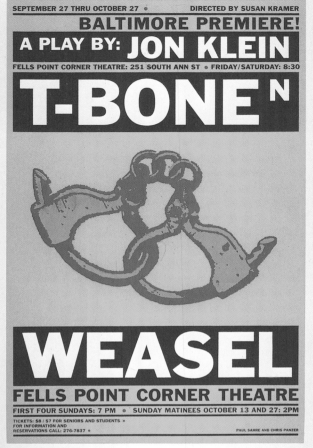

SEPTEMBER 27 THRU OCTOBER 27 • DIRECTED BY SUSAN KRAMER

BALTIMORE PREMIERE!

A PLAY BY: JON KLEIN

FELLS POINT CORNER THEATRE: 251 SOUTH ANN ST • FRIDAY/SATURDAY: 8:30

T-BONE^N

WEASEL

FELLS POINT CORNER THEATRE

FIRST FOUR SUNDAYS: 7 PM • SUNDAY MATINEES OCTOBER 13 AND 27: 2PM

TICKETS: $8 / $7 FOR SENIORS AND STUDENTS •
FOR INFORMATION AND
RESERVATIONS CALL: 276-7837 •

PAUL SAHRE AND CHRIS PANZER

PS

58

THE BALTIMORE PLAYWRIGHTS FESTIVAL
10th ANNIVERSARY.

ALLEY

AN ORIGINAL PLAY by: HERMAN KEMPER

APPLES

DIRECTED BY RICHARD B. JACKSON
* FELLS POINT CORNER THEATRE
521 SOUTH ANN STREET
(TICKETS: $7/ $6 FOR SENIORS & STUDENTS)
INFORMATION + RESERVATIONS 276-7837

AUGUST 9 — AUGUST 25
FRI/SAT 8:30PM + SUN 7PM.

POSTER DESIGN & PRINTING BY PAUL SAHRE & CHRIS PANZER.

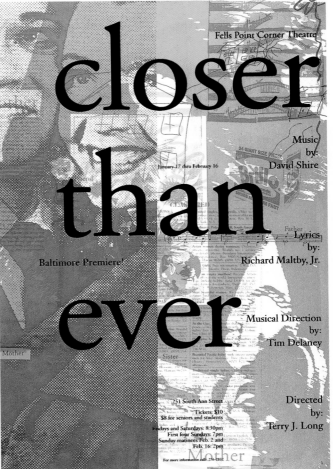

Fells Point Corner Theatre

closer
than
ever

January 17 thru February 16

Baltimore Premiere!

Music by:
David Shire

Lyrics by:
Richard Maltby, Jr.

Musical Direction by:
Tim Delaney

Directed by:
Terry J. Long

251 South Ann Street
Tickets: $10
$8 for seniors and students
Fridays and Saturdays: 8:30pm
First four Sundays: 7pm
Sunday matinees Feb. 2 and
Feb. 16: 2pm
For more information call: 276-7837

SAHRE

Once I got my silkscreen studio up and running, I looked for a client I could do some poster work for. I found the Fells Point Corner Theatre, a not-for-profit, 75-seat theatre. I began designing and printing this series of posters for them, charging them for materials only. This ended up being $100 to $150 for 100 handprinted posters.

This body of work led me to the book jacket design that I'm doing now. Art directors at New York publishing houses who had seen the posters started calling me with jacket assignments. And so I was kind of pulled to New York.

With my book jackets, I try to allow the solutions to stem from the content of the book, so I wanted to be equally involved at the theatre. I sat in on read-throughs, went to rehearsals, talked with the director, and read each play.

Tiny Alice is a play about Catholicism and the Church. The T's, because of a change of typeface, become crosses.

Good was an interesting play about a German doctor who, during the course of the play, joins (or is forced to join) the Nazi party and eventually becomes director of Auschwitz, and all the time he's trying to convince himself that he's doing the right thing, that he's doing good. This is definitely one of those occasions where I felt that the best idea didn't end up happening in the end. Originally I wanted the poster to be a big picture of Hitler with the word "Good" on it. But the theatre was really skittish about neo-Nazis or protestors. They were really paranoid, and they felt like something bad would happen if they posted that solution around Baltimore. I like what we ended up with and all, but what a lost opportunity.

PS

Fells Point Corner Theatre 276-7837

play by: C P Taylor

director: Barry Feinstein

Good

march 12 → april 18

Baltimore Premiere!

PS

FELLS POINT CORNER THEATRE

Directed by: Steve Goldklang

BABY WITH THE BATHWATER

BY: CHRISTOPHER DURANG

SEPT 18–OCT 25

Reservations 276-7837

Fells Point Corner Theatre: 251 S. Ann St.

Admission: $9/$8 seniors and students.

Fridays + Saturdays 8:30 pm   Sundays at 2 pm

PS

This poster they didn't like: *Abstract Purple.*
They felt it didn't work well on the street,
and I guess I agree with their criticism. But
as it turns out it's one of my favorite posters
of the series.

   You'd think that I had a great working
relationship with the theatre—usually when
I show these posters people say, "They must
have loved you." They did, and they didn't. I
was kind of a pain in the ass to them.
Nothing was ever readable enough, they
were always saying, "Do you have to break
up the headline like that?" or, "We can't
read it"—you know, typical client stuff. And
since I was doing this for free and printing it
as well.... So all that was in the mix. It was
kind of interesting—after a while it was kind
of this running joke that they would always
hate the one I'd just delivered, then when I'd
design the next one, they'd always ask why
it wasn't as good as the last one—you know,
the one they didn't like and couldn't read. I
guess after they started using each poster
they always came around and were happy
with them in the end. But it never seemed
like it when I was doing them, which was
a drag.

These posters are all very graphic and pretty
simple. Part of that certainly has to do with
the printing process. As the designer *and*
printer, I've simply got to be able to print it.
And I would definitely consider myself a
novice silkscreener compared to someone
who does it for a living, and I had very limited resources as you saw before. So a lot of
times I would mess up the design of something just so it would be easier to print. This
poster, *Italian American Reconciliation,* was
difficult to print because I'm holding 10-
point Bodoni and good registration was
important.

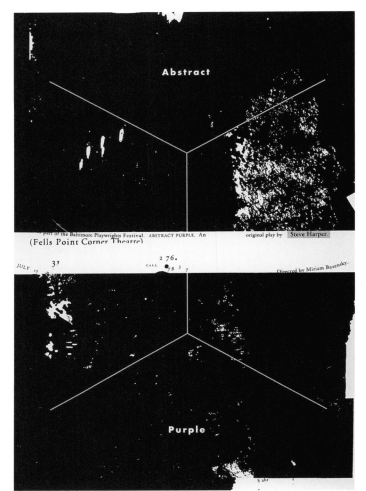

PS

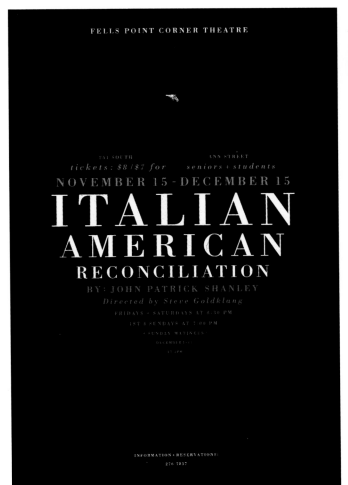

FELLS POINT CORNER THEATRE

251 SOUTH   ANN STREET

tickets: $8 / $7 for   *seniors + students*

NOVEMBER 15 - DECEMBER 15

ITALIAN
AMERICAN
RECONCILIATION

BY: JOHN PATRICK SHANLEY

Directed by Steve Goldklang

FRIDAYS + SATURDAYS AT 8:30 PM

1ST 4 SUNDAYS AT 7:00 PM

+ SUNDAY MATINEES

DECEMBER 1 +

17 2PM

INFORMATION + RESERVATIONS:

276-7837

PS

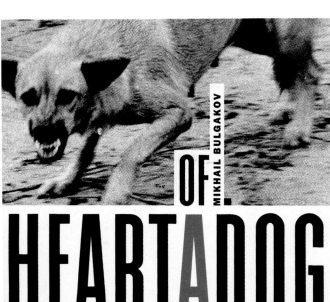

MIKHAIL BULGAKOV

OF
HEARTADOG

MARCH 13 THRU APRIL 12

ADAPTED BY: FRANK GALATI
DIRECTED BY: RICHARD JACKSON

RESERVATIONS:

276
-7837

251 S.
ANN
ST.

FELLS POINT
CORNER THEATRE

TICKETS: $8
$7 FOR SENIORS
& STUDENTS

BALTIMORE PREMIERE!

1ST 4 SUNDAYS: 7 PM
SUNDAY MATINEES:
MAR. 29 & APR. 12: 2 PM

FRIDAYS & SATURDAYS: 8:30 PM

PS

63

SAHRE

This one, *Love and Anger,* was very easy to print. There was very little waste. If something was off-register it didn't matter.

This is another one that was very difficult to print, *Ghosts Play One,* because of the 8-point Garamond. This is one of those cases, too, where I dropped off the posters and a day later I got a call from the chairwoman who said, "There's a problem with the posters." I asked her what the problem was and she said, "The name of the theatre is crossed out."

(a cell phone rings)

The Fever is a play by Wallace Shawn. It's about a man getting sick on the bathroom floor. The entire play is a monologue. Here's an instance where I found an image and appropriated it, hopefully creating something new by changing the context and by cropping. The image is news photograph of one of the American hostages in Iran. Due to the crop, etc., it becomes something ambiguous and, I think, pretty interesting. The new image is definitely more open-ended.

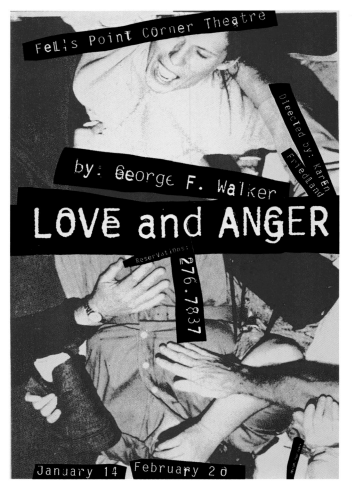

PS

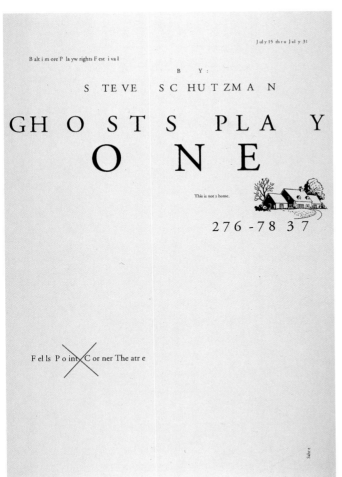

These next two posters illustrate one of the difficulties of doing pro-bono work for a client. Over the five years I worked with the theatre, I collaborated with several designers, most often with David Plunkert. This was great for a couple reasons: the collaboration kept the designs fresh, and I had someone to help me with the printing.

This was an image David did for a play called *Camisado* (right). Metaphorically, this play was about masks. The main character (a woman) is having an affair, and the play deals with the ways in which we hide or reveal ourselves. The theatre didn't like this poster. We told them that we really felt it worked and they could take it or leave it, thinking they might have a change of heart if given an ultimatum. But they left it, and this is what they ended up doing instead (opposite). They were so strongly against our poster that they passed on a handmade, silkscreened print for an 11" x 17" Xerox that they did themselves. This is really the kind of poster they were using before I came along and, you know, in the end I think they were much happier with this. They got to put their logo and photos of the actors on the poster, which I was always fighting against.

PS

Fells Point Corner Theatre

AND

THE BALTIMORE PLAYWRIGHTS FESTIVAL

PRESENTS KATHLEEN BARBER'S

C A M I S A D O

DIRECTED BY

ROBERT CLINGAN

AUGUST 13-SEPTEMBER 5

FRIDAYS/SATURDAYS AT 8:30 P.M.
SUNDAYS AT 7:00 P.M.

FP CT

FELLS POINT CORNER THEATRE
251 South Ann Street
Baltimore, Maryland 21231

ADMISSION: GENERAL $9.00   SENIORS/STUDENTS $8.00
FOR INFORMATION AND RESERVATIONS, CALL THE THEATRE:

(410) 276-7837

SAHRE

You've really got to *want* to do posters, always being on the alert for opportunities. This is a poster/invitation for my dog's first-birthday party, which I printed.

Another thing about silkscreen—it can allow you to make your ideas happen. These are 30-foot billboard sheets (top row). I printed an opaque white and gold circle and a "PS." I also added a cut line that says, "A by-product of the Design Office of Paul Sahre." I give these to clients, trade them with other designers (I collect posters so I'm doing that quite often), hang them in my studio, etc. There's an applied aspect of it that I also feel is nonapplied, so I don't know if this is still graphic design.

I also do some work that isn't applied at all. For instance, I buy wood scenes at souvenir shops and silkscreen words on top of them (pages 70–71). The words all have to do with expulsion or being kicked out or leaving perfect places. I feel so far away from any of these places. Let's just say that none of these views are anything like the view from my apartment in Brooklyn. Actually, I don't even have a view from my studio in Manhattan, where there aren't any windows.

PS

PS

PS

NG CANCER

PS

oust

dismiss

vacate

abandon

SAHRE

I brew my own beer: "Pop-Skull."
I did a label with a skull and cross bones
on one side and Mr. Brady on the other,
and gave my beer as a Christmas gift
(right). I also sent bottles in to few
design compitions. I got a call from Carol
Waller at the Type Directors club a few
weeks after the show opened, and it turns
out that my bottle of home brew had
exploded all over the other entries.

I don't send homebrew to design
compitions anymore.

This is my marriage license (opposite). I got
divorced about four years ago. I printed a big
red square over my marriage certificate. And
then put it into one of those certificate
frames.

Very, very satisfying.

PS

72

For their 50th anniversary, Farrar, Straus & Giroux asked fifty designers to do a fish (their logo is three fish). And this one of a booby-trapped fish really stood out (right). I thought it was so subversive. I called designer/friend James Victore and asked, Who is this guy? And he said, Oh, that's Paul Sahre, he's a designer from Baltimore, he's great. And he's a thinker—meaning that Paul believes in the supremacy of the idea.

I always have a tough time explaining my leap from an underground comix magazine that no one would ever see, to the Op-Ed page of the *New York Times*, something everyone would see. I had shown a few copies of *Nozone* to Steven Heller, art director of the *New York Times Book Review*, and when the *Times* was understaffed, when an art director was sick or on vacation, he suggested I fill in. And people at the *Times* would ask, "What does Blechman know about art direction?" and Heller answered, "He does *Nozone*, so he must know a lot of illustrators." And the bulk of the images for the Op-Ed page was illustration. So they hired me.

This is your traditional Op-Ed page illustration: concept-driven black-and-white line art—executed within 24 hours (opposite).

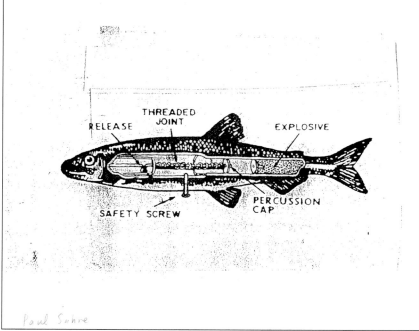

PS

My father, R.O. Blechman, did this drawing (right). Everything I ever learned about graphic design came from my father, and here I was art directing him. I remember as a kid looking at the *Times* every morning and being fascinated by the front page with its dramatic headlines and grainy news photos. I even remember going to the *Times* with my father when he was under deadline. Once he was having problems drawing a water droplet and asked me to help him. So I drew a droplet and he took it and pasted it on his drawing and that's how I got my first drawing published.

The Op-Ed page has traditionally been the turf of an elite group of illustrators. I have varied that by giving assignments to graphic designers to see how they would solve the same problems: instead of collage, photography; instead of a drawing, an icon; instead of a cartoon bubble, typography.

    This is a piece asking Congress to cut funding for the National Endowment for the Arts (opposite). I called Paul Rand, who sent me a strange fax of a clown.

    "What's this? I don't get it," I said.

    "It's a clown," he said.

    "Why a clown?"

    "Because it's a joke, the whole thing's a joke, the NEA's a joke!"

    "Well, do you have any other ideas?"

    "The only other thing I can do in this amount of time [two hours] is take the letters N-E-A and rip 'em up."

    "Let me think about it."

    Unsure of this idea, I called my father, who said, "If Paul Rand wants to tear up the letters N-E-A then it won't be like anyone else tearing them up. Just make sure he signs it."

NB

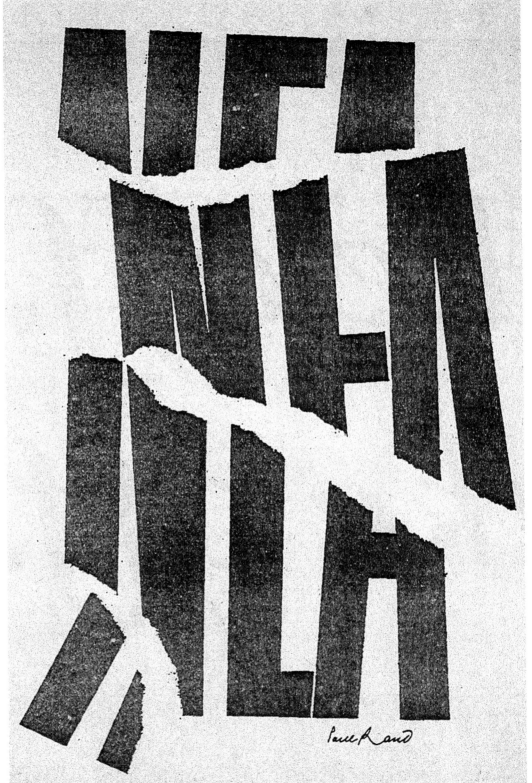

My dream for the Op-Ed page was to have the art exist independently of the articles, as a stand-alone, making its own editorial comment. And so we came up with a category called Op-Art.

One of the early Op-Arts was a proposal for generic cigarette packaging by Tibor Kalman (right). The other piece is by Jules Feiffer (opposite).

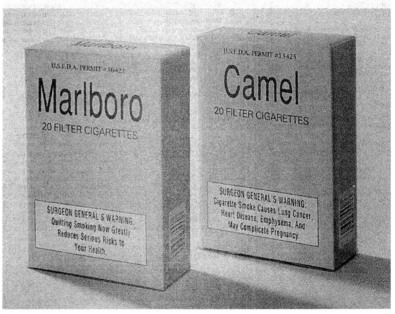

NB

BLECHMAN

This piece by Barbara Kruger was accompanied by editorials on the future of the
Internet.

The future belongs to those who can see it

BLECHMAN

There are two different ways to solve an Op-Ed: one is to put a square illustration in the middle of the type; the other is to think about how the whole page works, as with this article on the history of New York City, in which the layout becomes the illustration (right).

SAHRE

That piece is crazy. I can't imagine how you got that done. As silly as it that sounds, as simple as it is, as an art director at the *Times* you don't have control over the layout to this degree. And you have to work with other systems and with other people on different floors and with a time crunch and with how the pieces grow and shrink editorially. I never try anything so involved with the layout when I'm sitting in for Nicholas.

BLECHMAN

There must have been something perverse in me when I assigned this piece on Coney Island to a typographer (opposite, left). It's perfect for an illustration; there's such a rich visual culture in Coney Island. But I thought it would be fun to see how a designer shows, for example, the Cyclone, using pure type. This was a production nightmare. We forgot to put the dot on the question mark and I lost sleep over that for the rest of the weekend.

How do you illustrate an article on the best quotes of 1998? Paula Scher took the whole article and put it in quotes (opposite, right).

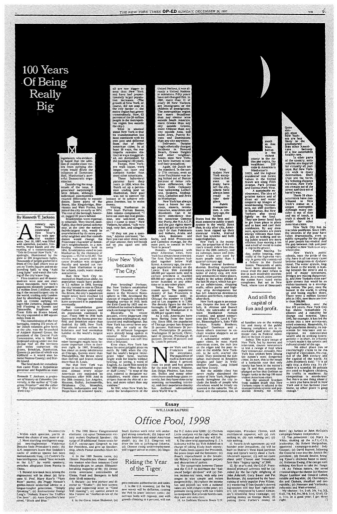

NB

NB

NB

BLECHMAN

This article was about doing politics online, digitally, and doing it in real time, offline (top right). For this piece we actually smuggled a mouse into the *Times* (animals aren't allowed in the building). The photographer was terrified that the mouse would get out and that he would get fired.

This photograph was for an article on deflation (middle right). The container comes from the Times cafeteria.

This is a piece on how humans are pretty closely related to Neanderthals (bottom right). We got a Neanderthal mask for Dan, the "actor." Dan loved wearing the mask so much that he refused to take it off. Even after the shoot, he'd walk around town with it on. He even tried getting back into the *Times* but security wouldn't let him in with it on. So he took the mask off and the guards took one look at him and said, "O.K., you can put it back on now."

Charles S. Anderson did this July 4th Op-Art at a time when India and Pakistan were testing nuclear weapons (opposite).

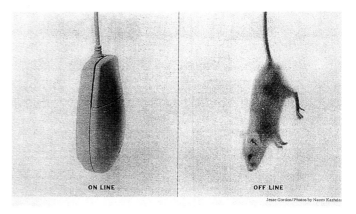

ON LINE   OFF LINE

Jesse Gordon/Photos by Naum Kazhdai

NB

84

Foreign Affairs
THOMAS L. FRIEDMAN

Jerusalem As Levittown

JERUSALEM

So the Israeli Government announces plans to extend the authority of the Jerusalem municipality over the hills and towns, primarily to the west and southwest of the Israeli capital. It says this is to improve city planning and services. The U.S. denounces this as a provocation that could derail peace talks. The Palestinians howl in protest. The U.N. moves to censure Israel. But behind the scenes, everyone is still asking: What is this Israeli move really about? Annexation? Provocation? Better bus service?

The answer may be none of the above. According to the Society for the Protection of Nature in Israel — which knows every hill, forest and stone in the areas to be brought under this greater Jerusalem umbrella — what this is most about is real estate development. We're talking Donald Trump, not Trumpeldor (a famous early Israeli pioneer).

For the past decade the Nature Society has been fighting successfully to limit development in the terraced hills and Jewish National Fund forests to the west and southwest of Jerusalem, explains Yoav Sagi, its chairman, who, along with Israel Kimhi, a former Jerusalem city planner, and Avram Shaked, the organization's conservation coordinator, gave me a tour of this area where Jerusalem is to be expanded.

"Right now much of this land is controlled by the state and it is designated as forest and parks, with some open spaces reserved for farming," says Mr. Sagi. "In accordance with the national plan, you can't build on these lands, except with great limitations. We have managed to freeze many real estate projects in these areas, to protect the Judean Hills, the parks and nature reserves.

"This move now to expand the boundaries of Jerusalem appears to us as an effort to get around these restrictions," adds Mr. Sagi. "It seems that the real estate powers are hoping that if the authority for development of these open spaces is shifted from the national planning administration to Jerusalem municipal control, it will be easier to get the restrictions on building lifted — because of the high cost of housing within Jerusalem's current boundaries, the influence of developers on

Why does Israel want to extend the city's authority?

city planning, and because of the political incentive to build Jewish Jerusalem. And once you get your hands on green areas like this, and turn them into real estate, you are talking about big money."

Real estate money has been known to find its way into political campaigns in Israel, noted Mr. Sagi, and some people are not above using nationalism to mask their real interests.

The Nature Society is fighting this urban sprawl everywhere. If you planted a tree in the hills between Jerusalem and Tel Aviv, visit it soon. It may not be there much longer, because by 2020 the area from Haifa to Tel Aviv to Jerusalem is likely to become "one big urban megalopolis," said Mr. Kimhi. "We build here like we are living in Australia — more is better, bigger is better," adds Mr. Sagi, "but we're not Australia."

It's hard to stop, though. If current population trends continue, Israel, outside the Negev Desert, will soon be one of the most densely populated countries in the world. This population explosion, coupled with the poor use of land inside Tel Aviv and Jerusalem — which results in these cities building outward instead of upward — is increasingly devouring the biblical landscape. The golden arches of McDonald's now dominate a prominent hill as you enter Jerusalem. If there were no Arab-Israeli conflict, the next big Israeli political party would surely be called "Green Now."

Israel can never limit Jewish immigration. But unless it gets much more sensitive about sustainable development, something essential to Zionism is going to be lost.

"Every project that is approved against the national plan, and destroys open space, destroys part of Jewish heritage — the biblical landscape of David and Solomon's day," said Mr. Shaked. "The Bible refers to the vineyards of Ben Shemen. Today Ben Shemen is the biggest highway interchange in the country. We still speak about 'The Land of Israel' in metaphysical terms, but we forget about the actual land."

Adds Mr. Sagi: "We have to change the culture here from conquering the land to preserving the land. Because if Israel should one day become a normal country, with no more wars, what will sustain us here is the quality of life and connection to the land. But if we keep to this trend, we will have no quality of life."

Journal
FRANK RICH

From Here to Zapruder

Whatever else you are doing in contemplation of America's birth this July Fourth, you will have to make do just a little bit longer without the Zapruder film.

It's not until August that all 26 seconds of this frame-by-frame record of the Kennedy assassination will at last be available to all Americans for nightly perusal in their own homes. Zapruder is going digitally with bells and whistles that Oliver Stone might envy: restored color in the grand manner of the new "Gone With the Wind," plus 45 minutes of added material guaranteed to inspire new grassy knoll speculations for the whole family.

The price is $19.98 for a VHS cassette, a bargain should by any chance the added material include commentary by the onetime J.F.K. supporter and full-time gun enthusiast Charlton Heston. The company bringing you this package, MPI Home Video, also distributes "The Texas Chainsaw Massacre," "The Honeymooners," "Dark Shadows," "Richard Pryor Live & Smokin'," "The Frugal Gourmet," "The Three Stooges" and "Liberace" — an all-American menu that takes one-stop

It's not all 'Yankee Doodle Dandy.'

shopping to a new dimension.

Perhaps Zapruder the Video will soon lead to Zapruder the Rock Video, Zapruder the Musical, or Zapruder the Fox series destined to succeed "Drudge." Such is the American way. If so, we shouldn't get too outraged about it. One of the many things worth loving about this country — and forgiving, when necessary — is its youth. America is in some ways still like that incorrigible kid you can find horsing around on the periphery of whatever cookout or fireworks display you happen to be at tonight. America is clumsy and impatient and uninhibited. After it falls down and scrapes its knees, it never tires of picking at its scabs and examining the wounds.

By the time "Zapruder" — or is it "Zapruder!"? — is at your local video store, it will be competing with some other newly repackaged cinema classics: the 100 best American movies selected by "1,500 prominent Americans" in a now-notorious poll conducted by the American Film Institute. It's not precisely clear who these 1,500 voters were. Bill Clinton and Al Gore — though mentioned in much of the press coverage — did not in fact vote, according to the White House. (This explains why "Lolita" is the only major Stanley Kubrick movie missing from the Top 100 — not to mention the absence of "Love Story.") Whoever the voters were, they've been deservedly reviled for dumping Buster Keaton, Preston Sturges and Fred Astaire in favor of "Dances With Wolves."

But the cineastes knocking one list miss one important point about it: As a snapshot of mass American taste, the AFI Top 100 does offer a revealing and representative take on our country's psyche. The movies listed as the best are certainly among the most popular, and they are often movies that hit us where we hurt. They are Zapruder films in the poetic, if not literal, sense.

Sure, there are some islands of pure pleasure ("Singin' in the Rain") and flag-waving ("Yankee Doodle Dandy") in the Top 100, but almost half the movies are violent. The most popular subjects include crime ("Double Indemnity," "Bonnie and Clyde," "The Godfather," among many others), the Vietnam War ("Platoon," "Apocalypse Now," "The Deer Hunter"), attempted assassination ("The Manchurian Candidate," "Taxi Driver"), urban dysfunction ("Midnight Cowboy," "Pulp Fiction"), marital infidelity ("The Apartment," "The Graduate") and race (from "The Birth of a Nation" to "Guess Who's Coming to Dinner"). The list's number 1 movie, "Citizen Kane," exuberantly describes the birth of the modern tabloid media machinery that disfigures both the facts and our understanding of all these issues.

What emerges over all is that cinematic self-portrait of a country more intrigued by its divisions and failures than its successes. We are aware (take it, by no rest "Raging Bull" and "China-town," both Top 100 films, than "Young Mr. Lincoln" or "The Longest Day." In the dreamy life of movies, we don't mind addressing what's bloody and nasty and unresolved in the American experiment. It's in real life that we too often lose perspective and think our deepest wounds can be healed overnight, as if we had no memory that many of them stretch back to the nation's infancy. But Americans have from the start been bigger in dreams than

Op-Art
CHARLES S. ANDERSON

FIRECRACKER Explosive SITUATION

CAUTION FLAMMABLE
USE ONLY UNDER
SUPERVIS

FIRST STRIKE!

JULY 4th

BOMBAY

INDIA PAKISTAN
WORLD'S LARGEST FIREWORKS

BOMB AY UNDER DOOR USE GROUND. LIGH

N? 8371 HJ
WORLD INSPECTION

POP

ATOM BOMB

TARGET

BOMBAY-INDIA

6pcs. FIREWORKS

WARNING — FLAMMAB
SEE BACK
FOR OTHER

DIRECTIONS : PLACE ON
GROUND, LIGHT FUSE, GET AWAY

COUNT DOWN
NUCLEAR TESTING

BANG

4
MADE IN INDIA

CHARLES S. ANDERSON DESIGN CO. MPLS. MN.

NB

NIEMANN

This illustration was for an article about the MoMA. The article said that the museum was haveing trouble defining what was modern, and what wasn't, now that the new millennium has caused confusion about "modern" versus "contemporary."

BLECHMAN

Paul Sahre did this illustration for the final episode of *Seinfeld* (bottom right). I still don't get it.

SAHRE

Nicholas doesn't watch a lot of TV. I don't either, but I had least seen a few episodes and knew what the show was about. He didn't know anything about it, which I think is strange but cool. Well, you know, *Seinfeld* is a show about nothing and it was going away. That's it.

Nicholas recruited me as a sit-in art director of the Op-Ed page. I consider the *Times* position as one of the perks of working solo: I can do things like this. The *Times* is such a different world than I'm used to: It's news, it's not about selling something, and it's a different way of working, too. When you're the art director you often have to be an imagemaker as well. Things change so fast—an article can come and go, and you could be stuck and have to do something completely new before the page closes. This is the piece I did for Rudolph Giuliani's second term as mayor—what New Yorkers wanted Giuliani to do in his second term (opposite). It became Post-it notes on the "right" photograph of Rudy.

NB, CN

NB, PS

NB, PS

SAHRE

As art director I get to hire people whose work I really admire. So I hire David Plunkert (right), I hire Jonathon Rosen, I hire Stephen Doyle, etc.

One of the other things I like is that it puts life and work in perspective every once in a while. For instance, I got a call from the editor one afternoon. She said that she had it on a pretty good authority that Joe DiMaggio wasn't going to last the day out, that he was dying. She said, You'd better commission an illustrator to do a memorial illustration so we'll have something for tomorrow morning. So I thought a minute about who could do a really important portrait of Joe DiMaggio, and Paul Davis of course came to mind. So the editor, Paul Davis, and I were on this Joe D. watch. It was one of these cases where you really have to stop and think about what you do—it's a very peculiar kind of feeling, anticipating someone's death with illustration or design. Paul did the illustration (opposite right), he painted it, and he emailed it to me. And the next day, Joe DiMaggio was sitting up in his hospital bed, ordering reporters out of his room. Which was very cool. He died two or three months later, and then this piece ran (opposite).

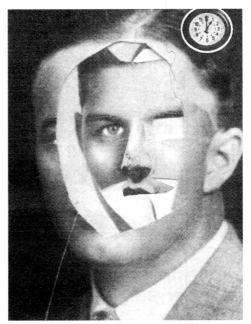

PS

88

PS

89

SAHRE

When I have a very hard subject to deal with I usually call Christoph because I know he will do something amazing and original, solutions that feel so right but that you didn't anticipate. And he's fast.

NIEMANN

We were just talking about the limitations of the Op-Ed page—it's always black and white, deadlines are tight, etc.—but sometimes I feel this allows you to come up with sharper solutions than you might if you had time to rethink your idea or consider the fancy printing possibilities (opposite).

BLECHMAN

The way this happened is, I often leave for the weekend and I can't get everything assigned before I go. So I take the Op-Ed piece with me. Whoever happens to be with me (and usually, there is at least one illustrator) ends up doing it. And that weekend, I was with Christoph (opposite).

NIEMANN

And we were drawing on weird pieces of paper over breakfast . . .

BLECHMAN

. . . pieces of scrap paper, whatever was around . . .

This was for the Letters section on the Editorial page, for a piece on artificial intelligence (top right). It's the lowest-paying illustration job in the newspaper. As a result, it's really tricky to find somebody who's willing to drop everything to do a small spot for $100 that's due in a few hours. But every now and then I get these little gems, and I think this is one of them.

NB, CN

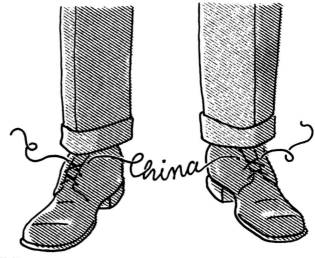

PS, CN

NB, CN

BLECHMAN

This is a piece Christoph did the day the Starr Report was made public (right). I think that what was difficult was trying to find a way to illustrate the events described in the report without being vulgar.

NIEMANN

The incident was all about one thing: sex. But the one thing you could never do was mention sex.

BLECHMAN

You had to find a way of illustrating what was going on without really showing it or depicting it. We were at a disadvantage by being imagemakers rather than word people, because word people can certainly describe it in eloquent or even clinical language. But it's very difficult to do that with images without it seeming ironic or funny, or down-right pornographic.

NIEMANN

Also, every day for five weeks the Letters and Op-Ed pages had been all about Monica, and you knew it would be the same thing for the next week and the next week. . . . I would just sit there and come up with more Monica ideas because I knew that Nicholas would eventually call again and request another one. It became like an exercise.

BLECHMAN

The challenge was to find a million different ways to illustrate the same event without repeating yourself. And this is one example of that: Monica as bait in a mousetrap (opposite).

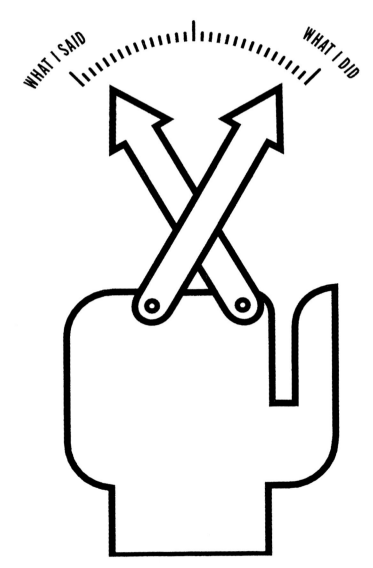

NB, CN

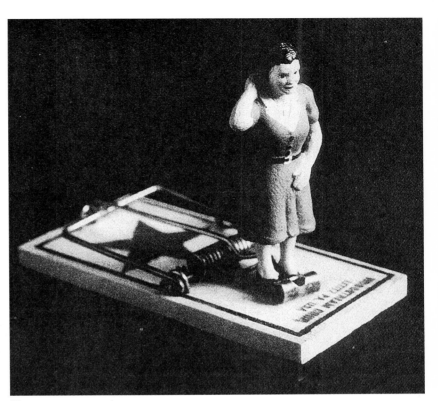

NB

BLECHMAN

This was at the time that the Republicans came out with ads attacking the Democrats for not impeaching the President (right). They were using the Monica Lewinsky scandal as a way to encourage people to vote Republican. We did a fake ad for the Republicans but there was a certain amount of confusion over this because a number of people thought it was a real ad. I guess the parody was a little too perfect.

Paul did this one: the Six Degrees of Monica (opposite).

NB

SIX *Degrees of Monica*

First came John Guare's play **"SIX DEGREES OF SEPARATION,"** with its theory that everyone is connected to everyone else through a chain of no more than six people. Then some college students with too much free time inexplicably began connecting the dots to the actor Kevin Bacon, and a small industry on the theme of "Six Degrees of Kevin Bacon" was born. Can "that woman," the world's most famous former White House intern, be far behind?

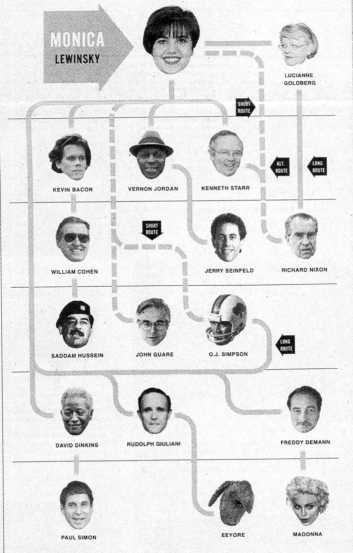

MONICA LEWINSKY

LUCIANNE GOLDBERG

SHORT ROUTE

ALT. ROUTE · LONG ROUTE

KEVIN BACON · VERNON JORDAN · KENNETH STARR

SHORT ROUTE

WILLIAM COHEN · JERRY SEINFELD · RICHARD NIXON

LONG ROUTE

SADDAM HUSSEIN · JOHN GUARE · O.J. SIMPSON

DAVID DINKINS · RUDOLPH GIULIANI · FREDDY DEMANN

PAUL SIMON · EEYORE · MADONNA

MADONNA for years had a manager named **FREDDY DEMANN**, whose daughter **NEYSA DEMANN ERBLAND** recently testified to the Whitewater grand jury about conversations she had with her childhood friend **MONICA LEWINSKY**.

PAUL SIMON created a Broadway catastrophe starring **RUBEN BLADES**, who is friends with the former New York City Mayor, **DAVID DINKINS**, who sits on the board of the Cosmetics Center, which is run by a subsidiary of the Revlon Corporation, which put forth and then withdrew a job offer to **MONICA LEWINSKY**.

O.J. SIMPSON (short route) lives in Brentwood, which is also home to the father of **MONICA LEWINSKY**.

O.J. SIMPSON (long route) was investigated by **MARK FUHRMAN**, who wrote a book that was handled by **LUCIANNE GOLDBERG**, who persuaded **LINDA TRIPP** to record conversations with **MONICA LEWINSKY**.

EEYORE will remain in New York thanks to **RUDOLPH GIULIANI**, who is a big fan of **PLACIDO DOMINGO**, whose sex life was the subject of a book by the self-described "glamorous Beverly Hills writer" **MARCIA LEWIS**, who gave birth to **MONICA LEWINSKY**.

JASON ALEXANDER plays a neurotic, self-obsessed New Yorker on a show starring **JERRY SEINFELD**, who appears in commercials for American Express, on whose board sits **VERNON JORDAN**, who arranged job interviews at the company's New York offices for **MONICA LEWINSKY**.

RICHARD NIXON (short route) tried to cover up a break-in at Democratic headquarters in the Watergate complex, which is home to **MONICA LEWINSKY**.

RICHARD NIXON (long route), in the 1972 election, trounced **GEORGE McGOVERN**, who flew around with Nixon-spy-masquerading-as-a-reporter **LUCIANNE GOLDBERG**, who (you know the rest) **MONICA LEWINSKY**.

RICHARD NIXON (alternate long route) was almost impeached by a Congressional committee that included Senator **HOWARD BAKER**, who is now part of the tobacco lobby, which is represented by a law firm that includes **KENNETH STARR**, who is making life very difficult for **MONICA LEWINSKY**.

SADDAM HUSSEIN may be about to be bombed by American warplanes in an attack directed by Secretary of Defense **WILLIAM COHEN**, whose top military spokesman is **KENNETH BACON**, who is in no way related to **KEVIN BACON** but who once hired a White House aide named **MONICA LEWINSKY**.

JOHN GUARE, whose play introduced this whole concept, once stayed overnight at the White House, which may or may not remain on the resume of **MONICA LEWINSKY**.

My mother, **BARBARA KIRBY**, once ate lunch in a Los Angeles restaurant that is said to be a favorite of **NANCY REAGAN**, who lives in Bel Air just down the way from **ELIZABETH TAYLOR**, who was dear friends with **NATALIE WOOD**, whose daughter graduated from Beverly Hills High School, which also matriculated **MONICA LEWINSKY**.

BLECHMAN

This papier-mâché portrait of Ken Starr used the actual Starr Report from the *Times* (right).

SAHRE

During this long period I would come in to the *Times* for a week or so and then I'd be gone for another month, and then I'd come in again for a couple of days. And of course it would still be there: Out of seven days, maybe six days had to be a Monica piece. And it just went on and on and on and on. . . . And this body of work squeezed every idea out of the subject matter.

This was the day the Starr Report was released. We wanted to portray it as a novel (opposite, top).

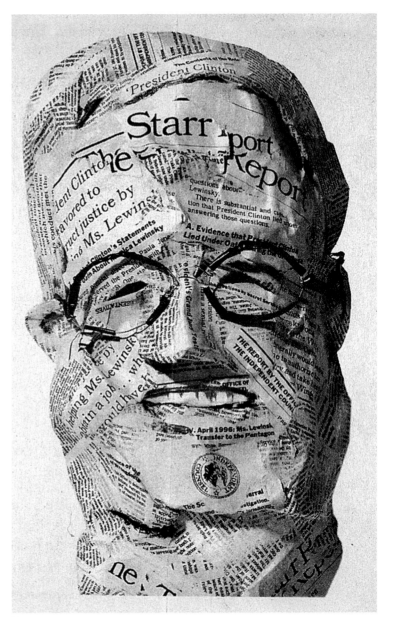

NB

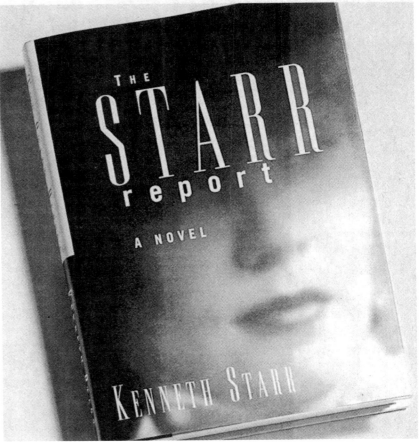

PS

Impeach ☐

Censure ☐

Enough ☐

PS

BLECHMAN

I keep a bunch of books in my office for emergency Op-Ed use. One was this old army manual from the 1960s for the signal corps, which Paul took advantage of while under a tight deadline (below).

Another challenging moment in art directing came during the Kosovo war. For days on end I would art direct nothing but Kosovo pieces. This one by Michael Bierut illustrates how today's peaceniks aren't protesting war the way they had in the '60s (opposite, left).

This was when there was fear of the deaths that would come from a land war in Kosovo (opposite, right).

NB, PS

NB

NB

This is the killed-work section. Killed work is really a part of what I do. Much more than I'd like it to be certainly, but it's—how can I phrase this in a positive way?—well, some work just doesn't end up happening for one reason or another. Sometimes it's client timidity, sometimes it's a matter of someone's personal taste, sometimes I screw up, but most of the time I think it has to do with marketing reasons—things that are really beyond my control. Whatever the reason, I end up with a bunch of work that I'm very happy with that has never seen the light of day. Plus, they've never really died if people can still see them.

I got a call from the U.S. Postal Service to design a stamp last year. I was very excited about it. This was to be part of a series of stamps on great American literature, I was assigned *Main Street* by Sinclair Lewis. These were the three different directions I designed and presented (right). I was psyched about the possibility of sticking my own stamp on my envelopes for a couple of years. But it died; the whole idea went away. It was really kind of depressing, but I was still very happy with the work I did.

A lot of my book jackets are killed. For *The Coming White Minority,* I appropriated the style of a type specimen page (opposite, left). I wanted a white, generic, European kind of feeling, and the type feels like it's shrinking. Also, it was a paperback cover and it's always difficult to do paperbacks because you normally have to work with these horrible quotes, but I really love the way I worked it in here. But often, when a cover is killed, I get another crack at it. This second design is the one the publisher ended up using (opposite, right).

PS

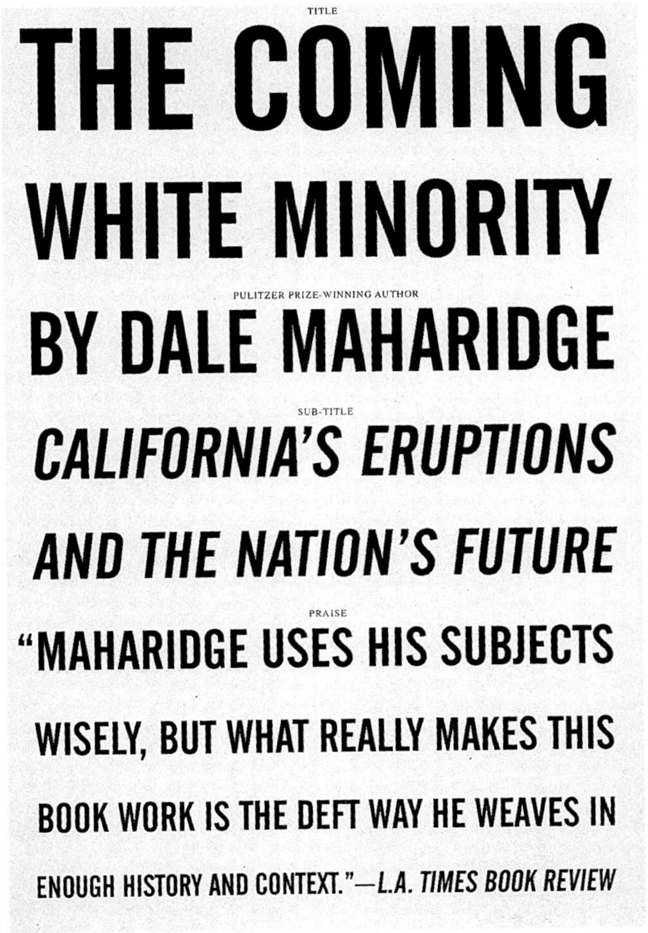

THE COMING
WHITE MINORITY

BY DALE MAHARIDGE

CALIFORNIA'S ERUPTIONS
AND THE NATION'S FUTURE

"MAHARIDGE USES HIS SUBJECTS

WISELY, BUT WHAT REALLY MAKES THIS

BOOK WORK IS THE DEFT WAY HE WEAVES IN

ENOUGH HISTORY AND CONTEXT."—*L.A. TIMES BOOK REVIEW*

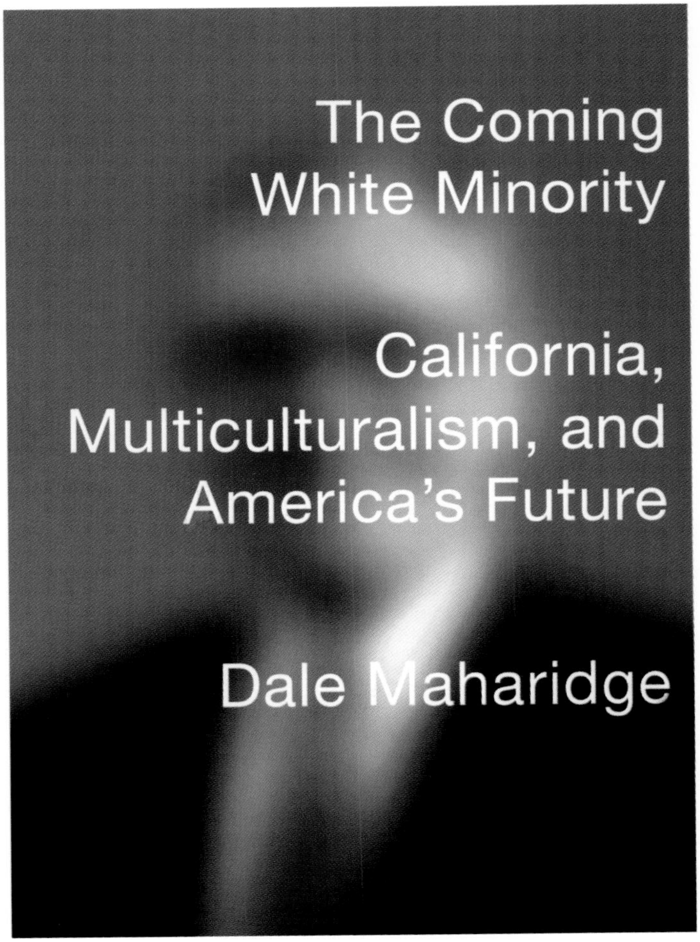

The Coming
White Minority

California,
Multiculturalism, and
America's Future

Dale Maharidge

Another killed jacket: *Plain and Normal*. I swiped an image from a clothing catalogue (right).

As She Climbed Across the Table is a very funny book about a woman who falls in love with a void (opposite, top left). She's an assistant to a scientist who has discovered a portal to another dimension. Somehow she starts assigning human qualities to it and eventually falls in love with the void and tries to get it to accept her, to swallow her. Very strange.

This is an assignment I might not take now (opposite, bottom left). I try to avoid this type of subject matter, for the obvious reasons, for political reasons—it's glorifying war—although I do like to solution. But the client didn't.

I'd like to give you an insight on how these projects can go awry and why they get killed. I got a call from an art director to do a cover for a book called *Willie* (opposite, bottom right). It's about a child with attention deficit disorder. The art director asked if I would be willing to work with an image they had chosen. I liked the image and accepted the job and applied the type. I did something very simple with it, a PhotoShop effect, to make it tie into the feeling of the photograph. The art director liked it—it was pretty cut and dried. I didn't hear anything for a few months, which often happens with book jackets. I finally got the call telling me the bad news, that the cover was killed. "Why was it killed?" I asked. "They didn't like the photograph," he said.

(laughter)

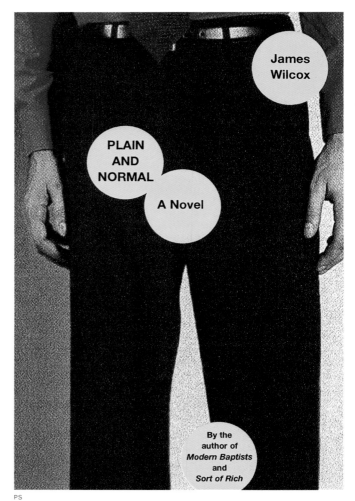

PS

AS SHE CLIMBED

ACROSS *the* TABLE

JONATHAN LETHAM

fig. 1 A

Exceptionally clever...A book of compelling ideas, of intelectual conflict, of human frailty and desire. And its funny. —*Dallas Morning Star*

THE

INSULT

RUPERT THOMSON

A NOVEL

BLIND MAN'S BLUFF

THE UNTOLD STORIES OF

AMERICAN SUBMARINE

ESPIONAGE

CHRISTOPHER DREW AND

SHERRY SONTAG

PS

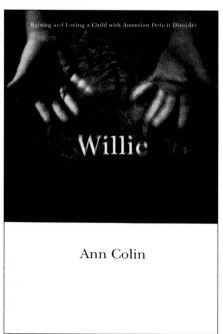

Raising and Loving a Child with Attention Deficit Disorder

Willie

Ann Colin

SAHRE

We're out of the killed-work now.

I do many different types of projects, and I like that aspect of working for myself. For Instance, I've been doing some CD packages. This is one for Verve, a re-release of some Spike Jones Christmas material (top right). I did a real campy/cheesy kind of thing with it. Imagemaking was really important here, and finding the right feel. I really like the music.

This is a poster for a book called *The Muhammad Ali Reader* (opposite). I had been assigned the book jacket already and, as I said, you have to look for opportunities to do posters, to make clients realize that they need one.

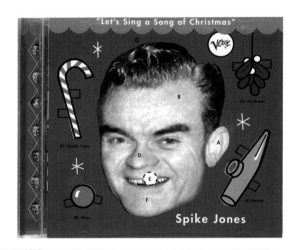

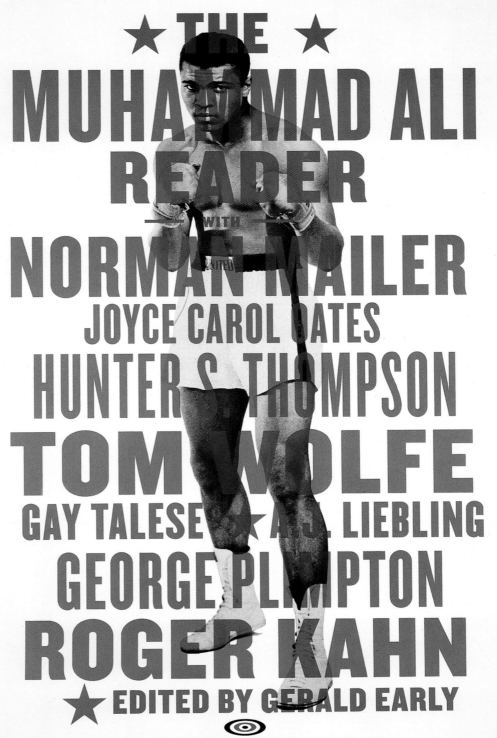

★ THE ★ MUHAMMAD ALI READER

WITH

NORMAN MAILER
JOYCE CAROL OATES
HUNTER S. THOMPSON
TOM WOLFE
GAY TALESE ★ A.J. LIEBLING
GEORGE PLIMPTON
ROGER KAHN

★ EDITED BY GERALD EARLY

ROB WEISBACH BOOKS
AN IMPRINT OF WILLIAM MORROW & COMPANY

PS

While in Baltimore, I designed several posters for the local chapter of the AIGA. I sent a fax of this poster to Emily Oberman and Bonnie Seigler of Number Seventeen, a design firm that specializes in design for television (right). I also faxed a note: "I hope you like the poster." The response was, "Which one am I?"

I designed this poster for Chip Kidd's lecture titled "The Kittens are Angry: Adventures in Book Jacket Design" (opposite).

PS

PROTECT

SELL

DECORATE

AIGA Baltimore Presents: CHIP KIDD "THE KITTENS ARE ANGRY" Adventures in Book Jacket Design APRIL 18TH at the BMA

Book Jacket Design

PS

SAHRE

Since moving to New York a few years ago
I've been doing theatre work again. This is a
poster for something put on by Crux, a production company in Brooklyn. It's called the
24 Hour Plays and the idea is that they get
writers, directors, actors, and set people
together at 10:00 one night and by 10:00
the next night they're performing an original
play. So the whole idea of the poster was to
make it feel like it was just thrown together
in a way. I designed the poster in a 24-hour
period as well.

A new client I'm very excited about working
with is the SoHo Repertory Theatre in New
York. It's an experimental black-box theatre
with almost no money to put into printing
and advertising. My designs for them
revolve around small, inexpensive colored
stickers. I have a great relationship with my
client in this case, artistic director Daniel
Aukin. The two of us are really in sync.

The logo is the sticker itself, and there is a
different sticker to advertise each perfor-
mance. We try to stick them everywhere
we can in the city. The sticker is also a
design element on each poster—obscuring,
adding to, detracting from, or interacting
with an image it sits on top of. The theatre
has have since asked me to become
involved with expanding their identity in
other ways as well.

SOHO
REP.

SAHRE

I curate an ever-changing window display in
front of the theatre. The first display was up
during the run of a play called *Cowboys and
Indians*. The window design is by Brian Rea.

I have also taken on the design of the theatre programs (middle and bottom right).
These have been a lot of fun. I use an elec-
tric typewriter and try to type and design
the thing in less than an hour and just have
fun, adding disconnected images, hand
drawings, whatever.

This is a poster for *Cowboys and Indians*
(opposite, top left). I love the fact that
there's just nothing going on here and that
the dot is covering up nothing.

For a play called *The Escapist*, this is a container that Houdini used (opposite, top
right). Again, the dot is interacting with the
image somehow in an attempt to define
something.

NIEMANN

This stuff hasn't got anything to do with
illustration, which ideally comes from a
graphic design point of view. But I can per-
fectly relate to the Houdini piece: I feel that
I completely understand it even though it
uses other media. For me this really shows
how the work that you and I do connects on
a certain level, even though it might seem
technically remote.

SAHRE

There is also an efficiency to this body of
work that I'm very pleased with. I'm pleased
with my level of restraint in the application
of the identity. I feel like this is the boiled-
down essence of what that theatre company
is about.

PS

PS

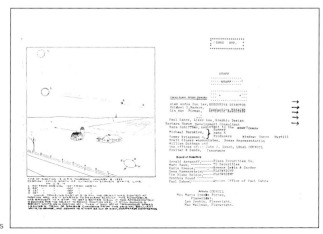

PS

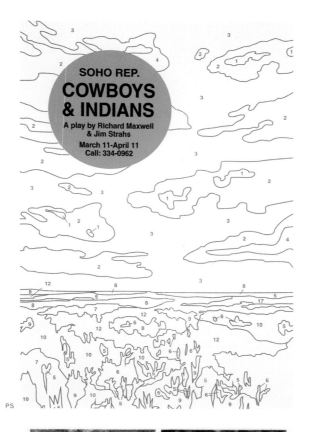

SOHO REP.
**COWBOYS
& INDIANS**
A play by Richard Maxwell
& Jim Strahs
March 11-April 11
Call: 334-0962

PS

SOHO REP. &
The Flying Machine:
**THE
ESCAPIST**
May 4-May 23
(212) 334-0962

Sahre

CHRISTINA
By Marina Shron
Dec. 1-4

**A 12 lb.
DISCOURSE**
By Matt Schneck &
Pete Simpson
Dec. 2,16

**CAT'S
PAW**
By Mac Wellman
Dec. 8-11

5
By Yehuda Duenyas
Dec. 15-18

SNATCH
By Peter Rose
Jan. 12-15

**A NEW
PLAY**
By Richard Maxwell
Jan. 19-22

PS

SOHO REP.
& SWEET JANE
**ALICE'S
EVIDENCE**
Concieved and Directed
by Ellen Beckerman
May 5-May 30
(212) 334-0962

Sahre/Tenniel

BLECHMAN

And this was for the end page for the New youk times magazine (opposite). This piece reminds me of christoph in its thinking: it's a sequence of drawings, all variations upon a single joke.

These are some samples of my illustration work, mostly done before I was at the *Times*. This piece was for *Slant*, a corporate 'zine put out by Urban Outfitters (top right).

A Canadian newspaper called the *National Post* commissioned this piece on Armageddon (bottom right).

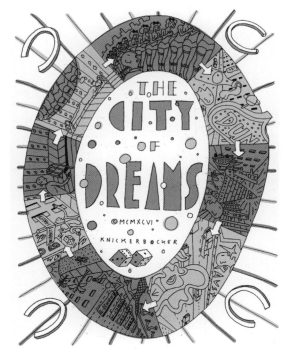

NB

NB

ENDPAPER

BY

KNICKERBOCKER

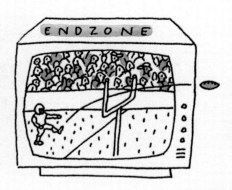

ENDZONE

ENDLESS

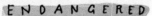

ENDANGERED

ENDTABLE

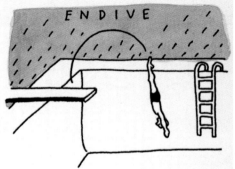

ENDIVE

ENDGAME

SAMUEL BECKETT

ENDORSEMENT

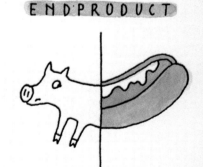

ENDPRODUCT

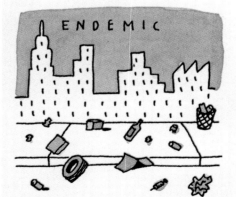

ENDEMIC

DEAD END

THE END

NB

When I'm not at the Op-Ed, I occasionally art direct *Home Design*, a supplement to the *New York Times Magazine*. This issue was about by how interiors designed in the '60s look completely different when they're remodeled in the '90s, even though the designers are the same (opposite).

And this was for the end page for the *New York Times Magazine* (right). This piece reminds me of Christoph in its thinking: it's a sequence of drawings, all variations upon a single joke.

The New York Times Magazine
PART 2 SPRING 1999

home DESIGN

Serial decorating: the evolution of taste

by Pilar Viladas

That was my first *New York Times Magazine* cover (right). And I was scared shitless when I did this because they gave me this job and I had no idea exactly what they wanted. They didn't really tell me until I got to the photo studio that I had to draw on this woman's head. The scary thing was that everyone assumed that I really knew what I was doing. It's pretty complicated to draw on a head because the material isn't really smooth and also the head is flat on top, but you still have to make it readable from the front. And there were ten people standing around me and I knew this costs tons of money and everyone was waiting for me to get this job done pretty fast and pretty good.

This one I drew on paper so I was a little less nervous (opposite left). It was a story on sex in the office and how it is not supposed to happen. And even though corporations like it when their employees get married, they don't want any relations to happen in the first place.

This is another *Times* piece, on Ken Starr (opposite right). That was basically the first sketch I did so I didn't even have time to become nervous. I sent it in and I thought I would have to do a final. They liked it but I really didn't believe them until a couple of days later. The little stroke there on the glasses, on the left side of the face, is the only thing that I changed after three days, after redoing the entire thing maybe twenty times until they convinced me that the original was right, that it just worked.

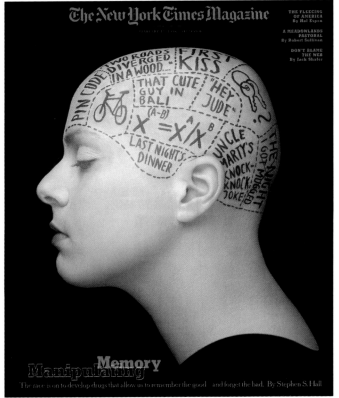

CN

CN

CN

This is a cover for *Print* magazine, for the new visual artists review (right). I hate to reveal my secrets, but kitchen equipment, in my opinion, is an abundant source of visual basics for illustration.

This is a *Book Review* piece on globalization (opposite). Besides kitchen appliances, the other thing that is always a good source for inspiration is maps.

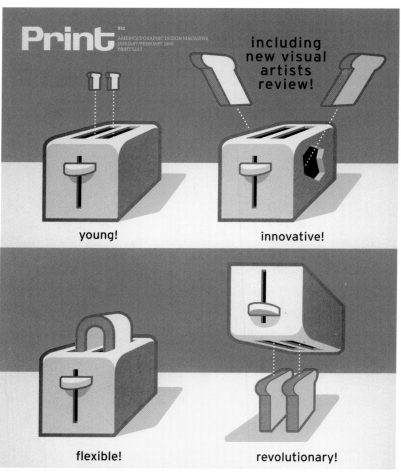

CN

The New York Times

Book Review

April 25, 1999

Section 7 Copyright © 1999 The New York Times

Whipping Up a New World

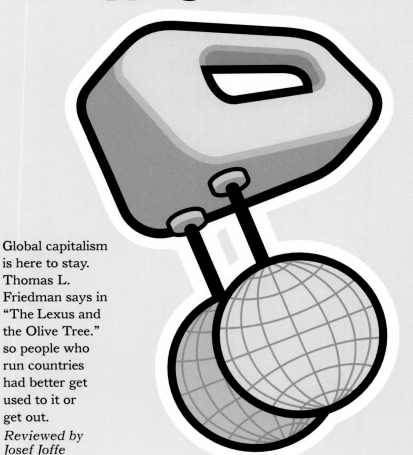

Global capitalism is here to stay. Thomas L. Friedman says in "The Lexus and the Olive Tree." so people who run countries had better get used to it or get out.

Reviewed by Josef Joffe

14

Global capitalism is immoral, unfair and unstable. John Gray says in "False Dawn"; its consequences, undermining economic intervention by states, will be terrible.

Reviewed by Fareed Zakaria

16

CHRISTOPH NIEMANN

NIEMANN

I did a book of paintings called *USA from Outer Space*. This piece is "Switzerland with Butter" (right).

Fortunately Nicholas shares my appreciation for maps, which led us to work on a series of books called "100%." It's very complicated. Every book in the series represents a portion of this 100%. That's *23%*—the revised atlas of the world. It's a silkscreened book on maps, of the idea of maps, and the abstraction of bringing this huge globe down to some lines and shapes and getting a better idea of these huge dimensions. And again, the more people know, the funnier it gets. There jokes are really about knowledge or the average person's knowledge of things, like that Wyoming is a square state.

SAHRE

Tell us more about the idea behind 100%.

BLECHMAN

The original idea was to do those 100 books never before published on the face of the earth. But Christoph said, That's too many books. The publishing company is called 100% and each new book is a certain percentage of that 100%, say 23%, 42%, or 6%.

SAHRE

I still don't get it. Can you guys say anything about the self-publishing aspect of it?

BLECHMAN

It was such a relief to be working on a project where we were our own client. If there is little distribution with *Nozone*, with 100% there's practically no distribution, and in a way that was really appealing. We would get together at night and have a beer and sketch out a few ideas and gradually put the book together. We did it for no other reason than to be creative (and drink beer).

CN

CN

YOU ARE HERE

THE REVISED ATLAS OF THE WORLD

23%

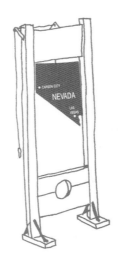

CARSON CITY

NEVADA

LAS VEGAS

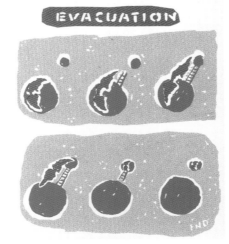

EVACUATION

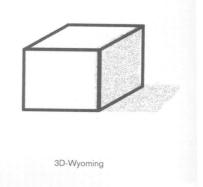

3D-Wyoming

CALIFORNIA

NIEMANN

This is something that I had always done—
making these little books. I like the form of
a book much better than just a couple of
drawings alone.

SAHRE

This piece is evidence of something I see in
both Christoph's and Nicholas's work. This
piece squeezes every possible idea out of
the subject matter. If you look at this book,
you will see that there are no map ideas
left to do.

BLECHMAN

Wait until we do the architecture book.

(laughter)

NIEMANN

This is a collection of images from another
one of the small books that I did before I
came to America (opposite). There's not
much to say about these pieces except that
I'm lazy and that I try to make graphic
design easy by narrowing down everything
to one symbol, which would mean that none
of us designers would ever have to work
again. You could just use these.

SAHRE

These are a series of pieces that are by-products of my silkscreening. A natural by-product of the printing process are make-readys, the sheets that go through the press a number of times to get the press up and running or to clean out something if there's a problem with the screen. The printer ends up using the same sheet of paper over and over and you end up with these random, disconnected images printed on top of each other. Designers have appreciated these things and admired them and collect them for years. The thing that was interesting for me was that these things were something that, as the printer, I could have control over, that it was my design that was being pulled apart and recombined on these sheets. So as I went I would try to loosely control what would happen—I would retire one after a certain amount of time, I would go through my stacks and see what would look good with whatever I was printing on that particular day. I just saved them and collected them. It's interesting, too, because I have a high degree of control over the work—and yet it can go totally haywire.

BLECHMAN

We cannot live exclusively off of commercial work. We need to operate at the margins of that. Paul does it by brewing beer and through his silkscreening, I do it through *Nozone* and 100%, and Christoph does it through his books. We all feel, I think, to a certain degree limited by the commercial constraints of our work. There is more to life than CitiBank, Random House, Young & Rubicam.

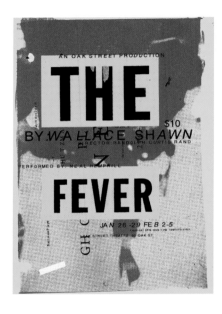

Paul Sahre

"Between the Pub
and the Private"

Mar

7 p

Sinclair Schantz
Center
Art Center Dayton

(937) 254-2711

SAHRE

Can I add something to what Nicholas was
saying about self-publishing? I think the bottom line is that there have to be different
reasons why we do design work. I never
want my work to be totally controlled by the
market. I don't always *need* a client to do
my work, or to make my ideas happen. As
far as that goes I don't need my work to be
applied, either. There's something very liber-
ating about that. That's kind of the essence
of why any of us does any of this. Because
it's for us, before it's for someone else.

Credits

x–1: Fresh Dialogue 1999; Poster, 1999; Designer: Nicholas Blechman, Christoph Niemann, Paul Sahre

3: Photography: Paul Sahre

4: *Omon Ra*; Book Jacket, 1996, offset lithograph; Designer: Paul Sahre; Creative Director: Michael Ian Kaye; Illustrator: Paul Sahre, Franklin Grippe; Publisher: Farrar, Straus & Giroux

5: *Couplings*; Book Jacket, 1995, offset lithograph; Designer: Paul Sahre; Creative Director: Michael Ian Kaye; Publisher: Farrar, Straus & Giroux

6: *The Theatre and Its Double*; Book Jacket, 1997, offset lithograph; Designer: Paul Sahre; Photography: Man Ray; Creative Director: John Gall; Publisher: Grove Atlantic

7 left: *Why Things Bite Back*; Book Jacket, 1997, offset lithograph; Designer: Paul Sahre; Photography: Edward Matalon; Creative Director: Carol Carson; Publisher: Alfred A. Knopf:

7 right: *Adopt International*; Book Jacket, 1997, offset lithograph; Designer: Paul Sahre; Photography: Michael Northrup; Creative Director: Michael Ian Kaye; Publisher: Farrar, Straus & Giroux

8: *Grey Area*; Book Jacket, 1997, offset lithograph; Designer: Paul Sahre; Illustrator: David Plunkert; Creative Director: John Gall; Publisher: Grove Atlantic

9 left: *Adultery*; Book Jacket, 1999, offset lithograph; Designer: Paul Sahre; Photography: Michael Northrup; Creative Director: Sara Eisenman; Publisher: Beacon Press

9 right: *Stripper Lessons*; Book Jacket, 1998, offset lithograph; Designer: Paul Sahre; Creative Director: John Gall; Publisher: Vintage

11: "Basic Elements of Nonelectronic Communication," 1995; Designer: Christoph Niemann

12 top: Designer: Christoph Niemann; Art Director: Gail Anderson; Creative Director: Fred Woodward; Publisher: Rolling Stone, 1995

12 bottom: Master P; Designer: Christoph Niemann; Art Director: Gail Anderson; Creative Director: Fred Woodward; Publisher: Rolling Stone, 1997

13: Prodigy; Designer: Christoph Niemann; Art Director: Gail Anderson; Creative Director: Fred Woodward; Publisher: Rolling Stone, 1997

14 top: Designer: Christoph Niemann; Art Director: Andree Kahlmorgan; Publisher: Business Week, 1997

14 bottom: Designer: Christoph Niemann; Art Director: Chris Curry; Publisher: *New Yorker*, 1998

15: Designer: Christoph Niemann; Art Director: Owen Phillips; Publisher: *New Yorker*, 1997–99

16 top: Designer: Christoph Niemann; Art Director: Steven Heller; Publisher: *New York Times Book Review*, 1998

16 bottom: Designer: Christoph Niemann; Art Director: Friederike N. Gauss; Publisher: *National Post*, Toronto, 1999

17: Designer: Christoph Niemann; Art Director: Steven Heller; Publisher: *New York Times Book Review*, 1998

18: Designer: Christoph Niemann; Art Director: Steven Heller; Publisher: *New York Times Book Review*, 1998

19: Designer: Christoph Niemann; Art Director: Janet Levy; Publisher: Parsons School of Design, New York, 1999

20: *Surge*; Magazine Cover, 1989, offset; Designer: Knickerbocker

21: *Nozone* #1; Magazine Cover, 1991, offset lithograph and web press; Designer: Knickerbocker; Publisher: *Nozone*

22–23: Illustrator: Knickerbocker; Art Director: Knickerbocker; Publisher: *Nozone*

24: Illustrator: Knickerbocker; Art Director: Knickerbocker; Publisher: *Nozone*

25 left: Illustrator: David Goldin; Art Director: Knickerbocker; Publisher: *Nozone*

25 right: Illustrator: Ron Barrett; Art Director: Knickerbocker; Publisher: *Nozone*

26: *Nozone* #2; Magazine Cover, 1992, offset lithograph; Illustrator: Gary Baseman; Art Director: Knickerbocker; Publisher: *Nozone*

27 left: *Nozone* #3; Magazine Cover, 1993, offset lithograph; Illustrator: Joost Swarte; Art Director: Publisher: *Nozone*

27 right: Illustrator: Knickerbocker; Art Director: Knickerbocker; Publisher: *Nozone*

28: *Nozone* #4; Magazine Cover, 1994, offset lithograph; Illustrator: Ron Barrett; Art Director: Publisher: *Nozone*

29: Photograph: Knickerbocker; Art Director: Knickerbocker; Publisher: *Nozone*

30: *Nozone* #5; Magazine Cover, 1995, offset lithograph; Illustrator: Mark Marek; Art Director: Knickerbocker; Publisher: *Nozone*

31 left: *Nozone* #5; Magazine Back Cover, 1992, offset lithograph; Designer: Knickerbocker; Art Director: Knickerbocker; Publisher: *Nozone*

31 middle: Illustrator: Knickerbocker; Art Director: Knickerbocker; Publisher: *Nozone*

31 right: Illustrator: Knickerbocker; Art Director: Knickerbocker; Publisher: *Nozone*

32: Flyer; Illustrator: Mike Gorman. Designer: Knickerbocker; Art Director: Knickerbocker; Publisher: *Nozone*

33: "Signs of the Time," 1995; Illustrator: Knickerbocker; Art Director: Knickerbocker; Publisher: *Nozone*

34 top right: "President's Week"; Illustrator: Chip Kidd and Calvin Chu; Art Director: Knickerbocker; Publisher: *Nozone*

90 bottom: "China"; Illustrator: Christoph Niemann; Art Director: Paul Sahre; Publisher: *New York Times*, 1998

91: "Totally Homework"; Illustrator: Christoph Niemann; Art Director: Nicholas Blechman; Publisher: *New York Times*, 1998

92: "What I Said/What I Did"; Illustrator: Christoph Niemann; Art Director: Nicholas Blechman; Publisher: *New York Times*, 1998

93: "Mousetrap"; Illustrator: Stephen Doyle; Art Director: Nicholas Blechman; Publisher: *New York Times*, 1998

94: "Republican Ad Proposal"; Illustrator: Jesse Gordon and Knickerbocker; Art Director: Nicholas Blechman; Publisher: *New York Times*, 1998

95: "Six Degrees of Monica"; Designer: Paul Sahre; Writer: David Kirby; Art Director: Nicholas Blechman; Publisher: *New York Times*, 1998

96: "Ken Starr"; Illustrator: Russell Christian; Art Director: Nicholas Blechman; Publisher: *New York Times*, 1998

97 top: "The Starr Report"; Designer: Chip Kidd; Art Director: Nicholas Blechman; Publisher: *New York Times*, 1998

97 bottom: "Impeach, Censure, Enough"; Illustrator: Paul Sahre; Art Director: Paul Sahre; Publisher: *New York Times*, 1998

98: Illustrator: Paul Sahre; Art Director: Paul Sahre; Publisher: *New York Times*, 1999

99 left: "Give War A Chance"; Illustrator: Michael Bierut; Art Director: Nicholas Blechman; Publisher: *New York Times*, 1999

99 right: "Bombs Away!" Illustrator: Art Hughes; Art Director: Nicholas Blechman; Publisher: *New York Times*, 1999

100–01: "Op-Ed Film"; Editor: Michael Blieden; Camera: Jesse Gordon; Art Director: Jesse Gordon, 1999

102: Main Street Stamp; Stamp proposal, 1998; Designer: Paul Sahre; Creative Director: Dick Sheaff; Client: The United States Postal Service; Publisher: Unpublished

103: *The Coming White Minority*; Book Jacket proposal, 1997; Designer: Paul Sahre; Creative Director: John Gall; Client: Vintage; Publisher: Unpublished

103: *The Coming White Minority*; Book Jacket, 1998, offset lithograph; Designer: Paul Sahre; Creative Director: John Gall; Publisher: Vintage

104: *Plain and Normal*; Book Jacket proposal, 1998; Designer: Paul Sahre; Creative Director: Michael Ian Kaye; Client: Little Brown; Publisher: Unpublished

105 top left: *As She Climbed across the Table*; Book Jacket proposal, 1998; Designer: Paul Sahre; Creative Director: John Gall; Client: Vintage; Publisher: Unpublished

105 top right: *The Insult*; Book Jacket proposal, 1998; Designer: Paul Sahre; Creative Director: John Gall; Client: Vintage; Publisher: Unpublished

105 bottom left: *Blind Man's Bluff*; Book Jacket proposal, 1998; Designer: Paul Sahre; Creative Director: Evan Gaffney; Client: Public Relations; Publisher: Unpublished

105 bottom right: *Willie*; Designer: Paul Sahre; Book Jacket proposal, 1996; Art Director: Paul Buckley; Photography: Rita Rivera; Client: Penguin USA; Publisher: Unpublished

106: Spike Jones, "Lets Sing a Song of Christmas"; Compact disk cover, 1996, offset lithograph; Designer: Paul Sahre; Art Director: Patricia Lie; Publisher: Verve Records

107: *The Muhammad Ali Reader*; Poster, 1999, offset lithograph; Publisher: Rob Weisbach Books

108: No. 17 Lecture; Poster, 1996, offset lithograph; Designer: Paul Sahre, Franklin Grippe; Publisher: American Institute of Graphic Arts, Baltimore chapter.

109: Chip Kidd Lecture; Poster, 1996, offset lithograph; Designer: Paul Sahre; Publisher: American Institute of Graphic Arts, Baltimore chapter.

111 left: The 24 Hour Plays; Flyer, 1998, offset lithograph; Designer: Paul Sahre; Publisher: Crux

111 right: Sticker; Logo, 1999, offset lithograph; Designer: Paul Sahre; Publisher: SoHo Repertory Theatre

112 top: Window No.1; Window display, 1999; Designer: Paul Sahre; Publisher: SoHo Repertory Theatre

112 middle: Window No. 2; Window display, 1999; Designer: Brian Rea; Curator: Paul Sahre; Publisher: SoHo Repertory Theatre

112 bottom: Program spreads, 1999, Xerox; Designer: Paul Sahre, Brian Rea; Publisher: SoHo Repertory Theatre

113 top left: *Cowboys and Indians*; Poster, 1999, silkscreen; Designer/Illustrator: Paul Sahre; Publisher: Fells Point Corner Theatre

113 top right: *The Escapist*; Poster, 1999, silkscreen; Designer: Paul Sahre; Publisher: Fells Point Corner Theatre

113 bottom left: *Research and Development*; Poster, 1999, silkscreen; Designer: Paul Sahre; Publisher: Fells Point Corner Theatre

113 bottom right: *Alice's Evidence*; Poster, 1999, silkscreen; Designer: Paul Sahre; Publisher: Fells Point Corner Theatre

114 top: "City of Dreams"; Illustrator: Knickerbocker; Publisher: *Slant*, 1996

114 bottom: "Second Coming Attraction"; Illustrator: Knickerbocker; Art Director: Frederike Gauss; Publisher: *Weekend Post*, 1999

115: "Endpage"; Illustrator: Knickerbocker; Designer: Lisa Naftolin; Art Director: Janet Froelich; Publisher: *New York Times Magazine*, 1995

117: "Home Design"; Magazine Cover; Photography: John Coolidge and Richard Bryant; Art Director: Nicholas Blechman; Publisher: *New York Times Magazine*, 1999

118: Designer: Christoph Niemann; *New York Times Magazine*, 1998; Art Director: Joel Cuyler; Creative Director: Janet Froelich

119 left: Designer: Christoph Niemann; *New York Times Magazine*, 1998; Art Director: Cathy Gilmore-Barnes; Creative Director: Janet Froelich

119 right: Designer: Christoph Niemann; *New York Times Magazine*, 1998; Art Director: Andrea Fella; Creative Director: Janet Froelich

120: Designer: Christoph Niemann; *Print Magazine* 1999; Art Director: Andrew Kner

121: Designer: Christoph Niemann; *New York Times Book Review*, 1999; Art Director: Steven Heller

122: Maps Paintings from "Everything Is Going to Be All Right," 1997; Designer: Christoph Niemann

123: "You Are Here," 1998; Designer: Christoph Niemann; Publisher: 100%, New York City

125: "The Good Shape," 1997; Designer: Christoph Niemann

126–27: Make-Readys; 1992–96, silkscreen; Designer: Paul Sahre; Publisher: Self-published